CHRISTIAN

The Trinitarian ...

20th Anniversary Special Edition

By

Nancy Chandler

The Christopagan Series

Azoth Khem Publishing
Huntsville, AL
November 2023

An Azoth Khem Publication

ISBN: 978-1-952880-09-4

Azoth Khem Publishing
29931 Copperpenny Drive NW
Harvest, AL 35749
www.azothkhem.com

Ordering Information:
Quantity sales and exclusive discounts are available on volume purchases by corporations
and others. For details, contact the publisher at the address above. For U.S. bookstores and
wholesale orders, please contact Azoth Khem Publishing at 256.221.5498 or visit
www.azothkhem.com.

Printed in the United States of America

Merry We Meet and Merry We Part:
The Trinity Dwells within Our Heart
As above, so below;
As within, so without.
As the Universe, so the Soul.

Bide the Wiccan Law ye must,
In perfect love and perfect trust.
Eight words the Wiccan Rede fulfill:
An' ye harm none, do what ye will.

What ye send forth comes back to thee
So, ever mind the Law of Three.
Follow this with mind and heart,
Merry meet, and merry part.

Blessed Be

*Dedicated to my mother, Dean Chandler, for
her endless love, inspiration, support,
and encouragement.*

Cover art: Ian Bristow

Illustrations: Brian Pitt

Contents

From the Author

Christian Wicca: the Trinitarian Tradition celebrated its 20th anniversary in July 2023. The journey has been incredible, uniting people with similar beliefs and promoting the growth of the Christopagan community.

When the book was first released, the title confused and overshadowed the tradition's name, "Trinitarian Wicca." The title had been specifically chosen to attract a particular group who wanted to explore Wicca and a Goddess-oriented Trinity outside of Church doctrine. Combining Jesus, the Goddess, and the Craft was taboo then. However, over the years, these factors have merged in various ways, signaling a shift in the conversation.

As we celebrate the 20th anniversary of *Christian Wicca: The Trinitarian Tradition*, I wish to honor the practitioners who helped to bring this tradition to life and the countless individuals who have found solace, inspiration, and spiritual growth within its embrace. May Trinitarian Wicca continue to thrive!

Blessed Be!
Nancy Chandler

Trinitarian Wicca Explained

Trinitarian Wicca is a tritheistic tradition defined by its focus on the Goddess-inclusive Trinity from the initial three centuries of Christianity before its transformation into orthodoxy. Trinitarian Wicca combines the practices of the Dianic and Alexandrian traditions of Wicca with the philosophies of the Greco-Egyptian Mystery Schools and the mystic recognition of the Divine Feminine based on Gnosticism and Kabbalah.

Trinitarian Wicca is frequently misunderstood as a modified form of Neo-Christianity due to the incorporation of the deities and mythologies surrounding the Biblical Jesus. It's crucial to recognize that practitioners of Trinitarian Wicca have consciously left behind the confines of the Church, embracing the holistic spirituality of Wicca.

At the heart of Trinitarian Wicca lies the concept of the Trinity. Throughout history, the significance of threes has captivated human minds; trinities and sets of threes profoundly impact human perception and cognition. Humans are naturally hardwired to think in patterns, finding order in the chaos and grouping them together. The number three provides a simple yet effective way to comprehend details and commit them to memory. Three evokes a sense of completeness, balance, and harmony.

We are surrounded by examples of threes. Human awareness is divided into the conscious, the subconscious, and the superconscious mind. Mind, body, and soul are the trinity of an individual's being. The triad of human existence is birth, life, and death. Humanity experiences life in the past, present, and future. Psychologically, trinities offer a sense of completeness as they create a beginning, middle, and end. This structure satisfies our innate desire for closure and resolution.

The veneration of the Blessed Trinity is a cornerstone of Trinitarian Wicca. This tradition's views on the Holy Trinity are aligned with tritheism, the theological concept of the Trinity existing as three separate and distinct Divine Beings. Each of the three deities of the Blessed Trinity is considered fully Divine and can interact collectively or independently of one another. These particular Gods are not seen as different aspects or manifestations of a single Deity but as individual, separate gods with distinct qualities and purposes.

The three Deities unite to create an immanent Trinity that permeates and protects life on all levels. The Blessed Trinity is part of humanity: the nourishing Earth, the life-giving Sun, and the reflective Moon. They guide us with a whisper in our ear, a random thought, and by the constellations in the sky.

The concept of the Social Trinity has waxed and waned throughout history. Tritheism allows humanity to explore the Divine Mysteries without being distracted by cognitive dissonance or confusion regarding what it means to be God/Goddess.

Trinities, or sets of three, appear in numerous civilizations' myths, religions, and spiritual practices, from ancient Egypt to modern Christianity. As such, trinities have a deeply rooted cultural significance ingrained into our collective consciousness, making them feel natural and familiar, passed down for generations.

Traditional Christianity recognizes the trinity as the Father, Son, and Holy Spirit but worships *God* as a single deity. The Father created all things; the Son is the divine incarnate who redeems humanity; and the Holy Spirit is the mediator between God and humanity. This trinity is perceived as one deity despite their separate roles.

In Hinduism, the trinity is known as Trimurti or three forms. This trinity consists of Brahma, Vishnu, and Shiva. Each deity embodies a cosmic function: Brahma creates new life, Vishnu preserves existing life, and Shiva destroys old life to create new. While each god has its own role in creation, they are seen as aspects of a single higher power.

Triplicities also possess an inherent aesthetic appeal that resonates with our visual perception. The rule of thirds, a principle in photography and design, suggests that dividing an image into three equal parts creates a visually pleasing composition. This principle is based on the idea that the human eye is naturally drawn to the intersection points.

Architects create a visually balanced and harmonious structure using three pillars or three arches. The aesthetic allure of trinities also extends to art, with history's most famous paintings utilizing the power of three to create visually captivating compositions.

Leonardo da Vinci's "The Last Supper" employs multiple trinities: Jesus and his apostles are arranged in groups of three. This arrangement gives the painting a sense of structure and stability while also drawing attention to each figure individually.

In Trinitarian Wicca, the Blessed Trinity is recognized as The Father/God aspect, a powerful, Benevolent Creator, and the solar source of life. He is the Divine Masculine/Paternal energy who watches over His creations with unconditional love. The Mother/Goddess aspect is equally powerful and embodies love, empathy, and nurturing. She is the Divine Feminine/Maternal energy who guides, protects, provides, and comforts Their children. Lastly, the Promised Child/Solar Lord symbolizes humanitarian love, kindness to others, generosity, hope, and potential for spiritual growth. The Solar Lord embodies Divine Knowledge and esoteric wisdom, serving as the conduit between the earthly and celestial realms.

Recognizing the Divine Masculine is essential, representing inner strength, wisdom, compassion, and protection. His balanced qualities are necessary for humanity to become spiritually self-aware. Without the Divine Feminine and a healthy, complete Divine Masculine, the Sacred Marriage will not occur, and a Divine Child will not be produced.

Trinitarian Wicca emphasizes the interactions of the God and Goddess throughout the Wheel of the Year while recognizing Jesus as the Solar Lord and the Dying and Rising God. In Trinitarian Wicca, Jesus is viewed not as a savior figure but as a Divine Archetype on the Hero's Journey. This approach allows us to understand the lessons of Jesus' spiritual journey as He combats trials and obstacles.

Trinitarian Wicca does not acknowledge the idea of Heaven and Hell but supports the concept of Eden as a symbolic representation of heightened awareness and reuniting humanity with Universal Consciousness. Eden is not a physical place but a state of being. It symbolizes the individual's attainment of the light body as we return to our purest state of being before our human birth.

Trinitarian Wicca rejects the concept of an external devil or Satan. Instead, we recognize the presence of the *ha-satan*, the adversarial self within. This acknowledgment highlights the belief in personal responsibility and the necessity for inner transformation rather than attributing evil solely to an external force. Practitioners work with their *ha-satan* to understand and integrate this adversarial aspect of ourselves, recognizing that it is essential to personal evolution. This is the Shadow Self.

Trinitarian Wicca emphasizes personal growth through self-knowledge and ethical responsibility to others and the environment. We cultivate wisdom from within rather than relying on external sources such as scripture. We honor our ancestors as guides to assist us in connecting with our inner knowledge, encourage us to access personal power in a balanced manner, and offer an understanding of cycles in birth, life, and death. Trinitarian Wicca allows us to be empowered by Divinity while still embodying human qualities such as frailty and imperfection.

Trinitarian Wiccans strive for self-awareness, to be present in each moment without being ruled by emotions or irrational impulses. We encourage newcomers to learn and practice meditation techniques to stay focused on their spiritual journey and connection with surrounding Divine energies. Developing empathy for others is encouraged to better understand those around us and to maintain a harmonious relationship with them.

Like other traditions, Trinitarian Wicca celebrates the Wheel of the Year: eight Sabbats or solar festivals, thirteen Esbats or full moons, and follows the Wiccan Rede: *"An' it harm none, do what ye wilt."*

This ethical code emphasizes our freedom to practice the Craft as each Wiccan desires. However, with this freedom comes the obligation that no one is hurt by the practitioner's decisions and behaviors. Harm goes beyond physical actions, verbal attacks, and aggressive confrontations that could result in mental, physical, or spiritual distress.

Trinitarian Wicca recognizes the natural cyclical patterns of life, death, and rebirth as part of creation. We celebrate Nature as a Divine manifestation, a conduit to our Higher Selves, and the source of ancient wisdom. By nourishing this bond, we reconnect directly without the need for an intermediary and create balance within ourselves. Achieving inner balance leads to a healthier level of productivity in our daily lives, whether at work or home, bringing love and understanding into our relationships with family, friends, and co-workers.

Trinitarian Wiccans revere the Earth's animals and plants and are mindful of how our actions affect them. We strive to live in balance with nature since all life forms are considered equal and worthy of respect and care. This ethic encourages practitioners to be responsible stewards of the Earth.

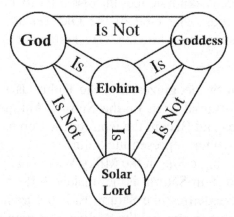

The Trinitarian Shield symbolizes the relationship between the three members of the Blessed Trinity and how they interact as a Social Trinity. Each circle represents one of the members: God, Goddess, and Solar Lord. In between each circle, there are connecting lines forming a triangle. This triangle represents the balance and harmony found in their relationship with each other.

God is not the Goddess, the Goddess is not the Solar Lord, and the Solar Lord is not God. However, God, Goddess, the Solar Lord, and the named deities make up the enigmatic Elohim, *the Gods*.

The recognition of Elohim as the catalyst of higher perception was instrumental in naming the Elohian pantheon, pronounced el-OH-HE-en. Elohim is the Hebrew translation for Gods in Genesis 1:1: *"In the beginning, God created the heavens and the earth."*

Elohim is both singular and plural. It is an enigmatic term, representing what humanity refers to as God. Elohim is singular when referenced as the Absolute, genderless, and all-encompassing. *Eloah* is the root word, feminine for *god,* in Hebrew; in English, it would translate to Goddess. The suffix *-im* is masculine and plural, indicating multiple deities, both Gods and Goddesses. It has been suggested that Elohim is a word like deer or sheep, used for singular or plural. However, this argument doesn't apply to Elohim because of its root word.

Trinitarian Wicca acknowledges the dissimilarity between the Old and New Testament Gods. The God of the Old Testament is jealous and applies strict punishments, while the New Testament God offers love and mercy.

Trinitarian Wicca recognizes God the Father as El, who is equated with Saturn, the original Sun, or the Sun of Antiquity. In the occult writings of Agrippa and Bacon, the icon for the Sun is a circle with a dot or diamond in the center, representing Saturn. Many texts generalize it as Sol or the familiar single Sun in the Milky Way Galaxy. Historians agree that the conflated Sun-Saturn issue makes little sense but evolved nevertheless. Unlike deities like Saturn, El is not transcendent. At most, El may be distant due to age and the decline of veneration. El is the chief creator of God of Gods, the Creator of Creatures. Recognized as the Canaanite Chief God, El presides over a Council that reflects his namesake.

YHWH or Yahweh is associated with the planet Jupiter. He is the Lord of the Ancient Living World and the tribal/regional God of Israel. In Gnosticism, Yahweh was considered the demiurge, a flawed deity born of Sophia, without the balancing energies of the Good Father. This instability causes YHWH and His creation to be incomplete and inherently evil. Because Trinitarian Wicca doesn't acknowledge external sources of evil, this tradition agrees that YHWH can best be understood as a God of Storms and God of the Forge. Yahweh or Jehovah's energy is still helpful for aggressive protection, retaliation, and combating enemies.

In mainstream Christianity, the feminine aspect of the Divine does not exist. The Goddess wears a mask in Christianity, appearing as a dove or a golden ray of light. She is called *Wisdom, the Glory of God,* and *the Spirit of God.* Though She was never openly acknowledged, many continued to search for Her under various names as a part of the Elohian pantheon.

The reincorporation of the Divine Feminine brings an understanding of inner power, which in turn brings comfort and fulfillment. The Great Mother's return fills the void created by organized religion for the last two millennia: duality is necessary for cosmic balance. The first step for most seekers is an epiphany that the Holy Spirit is the Goddess.

When you make the connection, this fragment of the *Gospel of the Hebrews* celebrates your epiphany! In this non-canonical gospel, this passage relates the relationship between Jesus and His Celestial Mother:

> *"And it came to pass when the Lord was come up out of the water, the whole fount of the Holy Spirit descended upon him and rested on Him and said to him: 'My Son, in all the prophets, was I waiting for you that you should come and I might rest in you. For you are my first begotten Son that reigns forever.'"*

> *"Even so did my mother, the Holy Spirit, take me by one of my hairs and carry me away on to the great mountain Tabor."*

Glimpses of the Feminine Divine in the New Testament become more evident as your studies progress. The Old Testament's *"Spirit of God"* is *Ruach ha-Kodesh* in Hebrew, a feminine gendered term when translated into English. She transforms into the Holy Spirit in the New Testament and becomes part of the Trinity. While She is portrayed as a dove or a golden ray of heavenly light, Her nurturing, wise, and comforting form speaks volumes.

Trinitarian Wiccans may interpret the Holy Spirit as a Deity in Her own right or as Sophia, Shekinah, or Asherah, the Three Wisdom Goddesses.

Sophia is a Gnostic Goddess who embodies Divine Wisdom, the source of knowledge, inspiration, and guidance. Shekinah originates in Jewish mysticism and is considered the indwelling manifestation of the Divine Feminine. Asherah is an ancient Canaanite goddess associated with fertility, nature, and nurturing.

The Virgin Mary has been the Goddess of Christendom for approximately 2,000 years. While not considered a Goddess by name, Mary's role is similar to that of the ancient goddesses, the Divine symbol of the holiness of womanhood. Trinitarian Wiccans with a Catholic upbringing may naturally recognize Mother Mary as a Goddess and the earthly manifestation of the Divine Feminine.

The Council of Ephesus in 431 A.C.E. decreed that the Church bestow the royal title of *Theotokos* upon Mary, meaning *"Mother of God,"* however, she was never considered *"God the Mother,"* the consort of *"God the Father."* In 1968, the Virgin Mary was elevated in the hierarchy of the Catholic Church. Mary was declared the *Mater Ecclesiae* or Mother of the Church.

In mystical Christianity, Sophia, the Wisdom Goddess, is acknowledged as the Great Mother. In the *Book of Proverbs*, She is known as Wisdom and is associated with power and understanding from God. Sophia is a mediator between humankind and the Good Father. Her qualities can balance one's soul by bringing together knowledge and wisdom in equal measures.

Sophia represents compassion, unconditional love for humankind, justice, freedom from evil influence, humility, hope for humanity's salvation through grace from God, and faith in His promises. She is an ambassador for peace, serving as a bridge between human nature and Divine grace while guiding individuals on their spiritual paths toward self-realization. Aspects of Hagia Sophia's teachings have been preserved throughout history by oral tradition or written scripture such as *The Gospel According to Mary Magdalene* or *The Pistis Sophia*.

The Gnostics speak abundantly about Sophia; the Greek term *sophia* is feminine for wisdom, and Gnostic comes from the Greek *gnosis*, which means knowledge. This time of knowledge comes not from studying scriptures but through meditation and personal revelation.

Shekinah is the indwelling of the Divine Presence on Earth, according to The Zohar, the foundational text of Jewish mysticism, or Kabbalah. She is the immanent feminine aspect of the perceived transcendent masculine. Shekinah is called Bride, the Sabbath Queen, and personified as the Daughter of God, the untouchable force inhabiting Israel. Early Jewish Christians acknowledged the Holy Spirit as feminine due to their understanding of Shekinah. She is the Divine Radiance that fills and sustains humanity and all creation. Shekinah's qualities include light, justice, mercy, and grace.

Shekinah resides in all things, both animate and inanimate. She is a conduit that transmits celestial energy into our physical realm, facilitating humanity's spiritual development and maintaining balance. When we achieve spiritual balance through connection with Shekinah, we can reach enlightenment and be free from all physical trappings.

Asherah and her daughter Anath are the primary Goddesses from the Canaanite roots of the Israelites. The "Queen of Heaven" is believed to be the Asherah, despite not mentioning Her name. These verses have been hotly debated by theologians and laymen alike. It reads paradoxically, making it difficult to know if this is Jeremiah speaking for God or his own opinion. Jeremiah 7:18-19 states:

> *18 But since we left off to burn incense to the queen of heaven, and to pour out drink offerings unto her, we have wanted all things, and have been consumed by the sword and by the famine.*

> *19 And when we burned incense to the Queen of Heaven, and poured out drink offerings unto her, did we make her cakes to worship her, and pour out drink offerings unto her, without our men?*

Archeological proof reveals that Asherah was once worshipped by the Children of Israel as the wife of their God, Yahweh. Asherah was a powerful fertility goddess associated with trees and pillars. Ultimately, Her worship was suppressed by King Hezekiah and again later by King Josiah.

Anath was also part of this Canaanite pantheon and is described as a warrior goddess who fought alongside Baal against Mot, a god of death. She is also associated with passion, sexuality, and fertility. Conflicting research says Anath was known as the Lady of Heaven. Others say the confusion is with Inanna, the Lady of Heaven.

The relationship between these goddesses differed depending on region; some were seen as wives or consorts to gods like Baal or Yahweh, while others were viewed as independent deities in their own right. These Goddesses have remained an influential part of Jewish history despite their suppression.

Mary Magdalene is an integral part of the early Christian story and a significant figure in the Gnostic accounts of Jesus. She was Jesus' most beloved disciple, the Apostle to the Apostles. In the *Gospel of Philip*, Mary Magdalene is called Jesus' companion or wife, repeatedly speaking of the disciples' jealousy when Jesus kissed her on the mouth:

> *"As for Wisdom [Sophia], who is called 'the barren,' She is the Mother of the Angels. In addition, the companion of the Saviour is Mary Magdalene. But Jesus loved her more than all the disciples and used to kiss her often on the mouth. The rest of the disciples were offended by it and expressed disapproval. They said to Him, 'Why do you love her more than all of us?' The Saviour said, 'Why do I not love you like her? When a blind man and one who sees are both together in darkness, they are no different from one another. When the light comes, then he who sees will see the light, And he who is blind will remain in darkness."*

Mary Magdalene is associated with the alabaster jar, and washing Jesus' feet with her hair creates an erotic image. The perfume in the jar is spikenard and worth a year's wages at the time. John 12:3:

> *"Then took Mary a pound of ointment of spikenard, very costly, and anointed the feet of Jesus, and wiped his feet with her hair: and the house was filled with the odour of the ointment."*

Orthodoxy depicted Mary as the penitent sinner who washed Jesus' feet with her tears and dried them with her hair. Nevertheless, Gnostic codices portray Mary Magdalene as a powerful prophet during the early Christian movement.

Mary Magdalene represents the Divine Feminine Rising, the reawakening of Goddess energy into traditional patriarchal religious structures. Historians suggest Mary Magdalene spread the Gospel of Jesus further from the Holy Lands than any other disciples, making significant impressions in Southern France. More statues and monuments indicate her ministry in the Gaul area than in any other country.

Levannah is an ancient Moon Goddess. She is not extensively discussed in modern interpretations of the Hebrew Bible except for Her significant references in the Book of Psalms. Levannah's role as a guiding light is revealed in Psalm 121:6, *"The sun shall not smite thee by day, nor the moon by night."* Levannah protected the Hebrews by night, as the sun did by day.

Levannah symbolizes femininity and fertility in Psalm 104:19, *"He appointed the moon for seasons: the sun knoweth his going down."* This verse implies that Levannah was crucial in determining the seasons' agricultural practices, creating the Wheel of the Year. The Hebrews associated Levannah with femininity and fertility, as the moon's cycles mirrored a woman's menstrual cycle. This connection between Levannah and fertility highlights the Hebrews' reverence for the Goddess and their belief in her ability to bless them with abundance and prosperity.

Psalm 89:37, *"It shall be established forever as the moon, and as a faithful witness in heaven,"* suggests that Levannah served as a witness to the covenant between God and the Hebrews. The moon's constancy and unwavering presence symbolize God's faithfulness and a reminder of *His* promises.

The legend of Lilith is captivating, and it is no wonder that she has been a subject of much debate. Lilith has been called the first feminist and portrayed by some authors as a powerful female entity with dark powers. She is viewed as a symbol of rebellion against patriarchy or an embodiment of feminine fortitude.

The Zohar, the foundational text of Kabbalah, tells us that Lilith was Adam's first wife who refused to accept a subservient role to her husband and demanded equality because they were created equally. In this regard, she can be seen as Adam's Siamese twin sister. According to Jewish mythology, they were connected back-to-back at Creation.

Lilith appears in various forms in mythology and folklore: sometimes, she is a demoness who seduces men in their sleep; sometimes, she is a beautiful maiden who tempts men with her beauty. Other times, Lilith holds court with demonic creatures. Regardless, She is an independent woman who never needs or accepts male companionship. Despite being vilified by patriarchal societies throughout history, Her story never disappeared from people's collective consciousness.

Lilith's power lies in embracing her femininity without submitting to a man's authority. Working with Lilith can help us cultivate our inner strength while maintaining our self-respect and autonomy, even when faced with opposition or domination. By embracing Her liberating energy, we can open ourselves up to opportunities we may have otherwise missed.

The Gnostics acknowledged a High Goddess named Barbelo, whom Jesus spoke of in *The Secret Gospel of John*, as the *"womb of the Universe."* Jesus also calls her the First Thought of the Unknowable God and the first knowable Deity. Trinitarian Wicca views Barbelo as the Star Goddess.

An excerpt from the Secret Gospel of John:

> *"For the Perfect One beholds itself in the light surrounding it. This is the spring of the water of life that gives forth all the worlds of every kind. The Perfect One gazes upon its image, sees it in the Spring of the spirit, and falls in love with the luminous water. This is the spring of pure, luminous water surrounding the Perfect One... Its Thought became active, and she who appeared in the presence of the Father in shining light came forth. She is the first power: she preceded everything and came forth from the Father's mind as the Forethought of all. [Barbelo] is the first Thought, the image of the Spirit. She became the universal womb, for She precedes everything."*

Zoe is a Gnostic deity and the daughter of Sophia. Her name means *"life,"* and she is known for her creative and life-sustaining breath. She is associated with new beginnings, transformation, and evolutionary change towards enlightenment and gnosis. Trinitarian Wicca acknowledges Zoe as Eve Ascended after eating from the Tree of Knowledge of Good and Evil.

Brigid is a fascinating and complex figure in Irish history and Celtic mythology, revered as both a Christian saint and a Celtic goddess, embodying her dual nature, various roles, and attributes. As a Celtic goddess, Brigid is associated with protecting livestock and crops, ensuring the well-being and abundance of the community. She is also seen as a goddess of inspiration, poetry, creativity, and education. Brigid is also depicted as a triple goddess with two sisters named Brigid. The three aspects of Brigid symbolize Her roles as a healer, bringing health; as a smithy, bringing strength and courage to the forged tools; and as a midwife, bringing new life into the world.

Following Christianization in Ireland during the 6th-7th centuries CE, Brigid became known as Saint Brigid of Kildare, where she established a monastery. Even as a saint, many of her Goddess virtues carried over into her sainthood through compassion, healing, protection, and charity. At the monastery in Kildare, She dedicated her life to serving the poor and needy and healing the sick.

Our Lady of Guadalupe's religious figure is connected to sainthood within the Catholic Church and to the Aztec Goddess Tonantzin. On December 9th, 1531, she appeared to a man named Juan Diego at Tepeyac Hill, close to Mexico City. Guadalupe requested that a church be built in Her honor on that hill. Despite Juan Diego's multiple attempts, the archbishop refused to construct it until Guadalupe gave Juan Diego a sign.

When Guadalupe reappeared, She told him to take his tilma, his outer cloak, and fill it with Castilian roses, which were not native to Mexico, as evidence of her presence. When he opened the garment for the archbishop, the iconic image of Guadalupe had been imprinted on it. The Basilica of Guadalupe was erected later, and the tilma remains exhibited there. Nevertheless, the Church declared that it was an apparition of Mary, the mother of Jesus, who had made herself known.

Guadalupe is associated with social justice and liberation for oppressed and marginalized people, especially women. She is usually depicted holding a scepter or staff, representing Her authority and strength against any oppressive forces threatening them. Guadalupe stands for spiritual protection, inner peace, compassion, and love for all who seek it.

When asked about working with pagan deities in addition to those in the Elohian pantheon, that is a personal choice. Personally, I set them apart. For example, as a cat person, of course, I cherish Bast for the protection of my fur babies. Likewise, I am a Persephone archetype; I honor that part of myself because it is an outside expression of how I tick magickally, drifting between Wicca and the study of ceremonial magick. I don't recommend crossing pantheons unless the collection of deities naturally crossover.

When asked about working with Jesus as Lord and Isis as Lady, I often give this example. Suppose a widowed American father with children of school age must remarry someone from Egypt. An example I offer when partnering with Jesus as Lord and Isis as Lady is the scenario of an American widower with school-aged children. He plans to remarry someone from Egypt, who is unfamiliar with the language, slang, and cultural norms of the U.S. Not only must she understand what type of clothing to buy for the kids so that they aren't bullied, but she also must master preparing healthy meals yet include some traditional favorites like pizza and hamburgers. Furthermore, she must understand her husband's workplace stressors and help navigate social dynamics within the children's schools.

Mary Magdalene and Isis share many similar qualities; however, it is important to consider practical applicability, comfort, and commonality when pairing Lord and Lady.

Trinitarian Wicca is a rich and diverse tradition, embracing the tritheistic structure of the Blessed Trinity and celebrating the deities that make up the Elohian pantheon. There is always room to grow; this tradition can enhance your mystical experience and allow you to think and feel outside the trappings of Orthodoxy.

The Journey of the Book

"What a long, strange trip it's been…"
"Truckin," The Grateful Dead

I was irrevocably drawn to Wicca. I was fortunate to be invited to public Dianic Wicca circles and Alexandrian guest gatherings while traveling with my band in the 80s. My experiences were beyond positive. These events transformed how I was raised to think about "God" and saved me from remaining completely irreligious.

Regardless, I hesitated to call on unfamiliar deities. I studied Greek and Roman mythology at a Protestant school. Their spin on the subject turned them into cartoon superheroes, which I could not erase from my mind or shake the "they aren't real" feeling. And I could not yet allow the concept of god forms and psychological archetypes to define "what was God." Despite growing up near New Orleans, with a heritage rich in diverse spirituality and folk practices, I could see the pieces of the puzzle dancing around me. But I couldn't see the big picture.

I read every book I could find on Wicca, then began researching Early Christianity, Jewish mysticism, and Gnosticism. Soon, I realized these faiths had more similarities than I had initially expected. As I delved into this project, I received helpful contributions from knowledgeable sources who provided me with rare books on mystical Christianity and Gnosticism to explore the marginalization of the Goddess. This was what I was looking for! Still, these scholastics weren't interested in applying this information to Wicca, and I couldn't understand their deliberate omission. Making the pieces fit together without further guidance was an overwhelming process; it was frustrating and isolating.

From 1999 to 2003, I devoted all my energy to studying these specific topics. Even though my university studies didn't include any religious education, my determination to uncover the historical truth never wavered.

Many people helped me to locate the primary missing Goddesses but were dismissive of my aim to incorporate a Goddess-inclusive Trinity into Wicca. To be fair, most of this group were Mystical Christians who embraced Sophia and New Age Christianity. Wicca and Christopaganism weren't their focus.

I immersed myself in studies at the local metaphysical church and learning center. There, I received a healthy exposure to the Theosophical Society, Madame Blavatsky, Buddha-Christ energies, and Alice Bailey's writings involving the Ascended Master Djwhal Khul. I was thrilled to discover I wasn't the first female to think outside the box regarding hybridized spirituality. Deep down, I felt like I was in great occult company! Nevertheless, their paradigm wasn't mine, and my strange compulsion to combine the Great Mother of Early Christianity into Wicca's framework was renewed.

Occasionally, I consider returning to college for comparative religious studies. Then I remembered that my beliefs didn't fit within one specific box—so why should I pursue someone else's path when I knew it wouldn't work for me? So, I bypassed more years at the local university and went directly to reading theology dissertations from universities dating back to the 1920s and 30s.

My research consumed my life before the release of the initial book—I neglected basic tasks like grocery shopping or laundry. Reference books were scattered all around my cramped apartment. I can't recall doing anything other than researching and jotting down notes. I was so immersed in the work that I had no desire to write music, play guitar, or perform with my old band. Everything got put on the back burner.

A profound sense of responsibility came with the information about the forgotten Goddess. Knowing that my book might negatively change someone else's spiritual views filled me with dread. My primary goal was to make the transition from the Church to the Circle easier for others than it had been for me and hopefully reduce any feelings of guilt. In hindsight, I wrote the book as a spiritual outlet. My pantheon of choice was not tolerated by most Pagan groups around 2000. Outside of the Christopagan community, my beliefs were not widely accepted, so I knew I couldn't be the only one feeling this way.

I struggled to write the first book and took everyone else with me. I drove my friends and family crazy with every step of my research. I wasn't trying to eliminate Jesus, but I couldn't understand why we had a Heavenly Father but didn't have a Heavenly Mother. I didn't understand why the God in the Old Testament was so cruel, yet Jesus spoke lovingly of His Father in Heaven. I was a fountain of questions running in a thousand directions at once, looking for clues to the forgotten Goddess.

I was raised in a rural Protestant church, but Catholicism always intrigued me as a teenager. While I never attended mass, I would watch the televised Midnight Mass at the Vatican every Christmas Eve. From the opening ceremony, seeing all the preparation that went into their spiritual routine was captivating. However, switching one dogma for another would not benefit me.

Televised Catholicism had such an effect on me back then. Now I know it's due to the elaborate rituals similar to the Alexandrian outer circle rituals, with robes, candles, the chalice, and the sensor burning Frankincense on charcoals.

While performing with my band in the 1980s, people occasionally approached me as I came off the stage and asked if I was a witch—which freaked me out! I had no idea what they meant, so I found a reason to excuse myself and dash to the band's dressing room. First, I didn't understand the question, and second, I didn't know why they would ask me this question.

Sure, I carried tarot cards, a bundle of runes, a pendulum, and a few oracles in my wardrobe trunk, but what did that have to do with being a witch? I never considered any of my collection to be a part of witchcraft.

My parents weren't too keen on liberal ideologies, so I assumed that if these items did have something to do with the Craft, they would not have allowed them in our house. My sister-in-law gave me an Oracle Book when I was ten years old. Mom bought my first Tarot deck at age fourteen, and around that time, I started to collect crystal balls.

Despite my obliviousness to my occult collection, the people who asked if I was a witch were the ones who introduced me to the world of magickal spirituality. I had never looked beyond my guitar for this type of thing—I didn't know it existed! For me, the mainstream Church was not engaging; it was contradictory and cold. This feeling led me to abandon it without even realizing it.

This changed after two Wiccan traditions converged in my mind. I could finally make sense of my spiritual journey. The Dianic coven was primarily Jewish. They included the Matriarchs of the Hebrew Bible in their practice and introduced me to Z. Budapest's writings. The Alexandrian approach to the Solar Lord's cycle of life, death, and rebirth opened my eyes to the parallels of my religious upbringing.

After attending open Circles, I realized everyone did not appreciate my syncretic vision. Several High Priestesses questioned which pantheon I venerated. I learned to remain vague: "I just address the Lord and Lady, God and Goddess." This generic version of Wicca had been used repeatedly in every book I owned, so I managed to go unnoticed for a while. Until I discovered others were skirting this question similarly. I realized I wasn't the only one, and it was time to speak up! I wanted to tell others that you don't have to fake being a "generic Wiccan." You can practice Wicca with deities you are comfortable with and do it in the Circle!

This silence and denial had to stop!

I reflected on my involvement with the Dianic group and the sense of community with those who used the term Elohim for God. It sounded musical to me; I am fascinated by foreign languages. Years later, when I thoroughly researched *Elohim*, I realized that more was happening. This Hebrew word for *"gods"* gave me a new feeling. It captivated my heart, mind, and soul. This new understanding changed my view of everything—ultimately, my life.

If we were made in the Gods' image and humanity is male and female, then the same must be true of what we have called "God." This term, Elohim, made so much sense to me, but how it remained unnoticed didn't make any sense. I couldn't understand why this plural term was used throughout the Bible when addressing the Oneness of God, especially in the Old Testament. This felt like a translation error or an editing oversight. Shouldn't someone have noticed this mistake in the last thousand years?

I began to obsess over Genesis 1:26-27:

> **"And God said, Let us make man in our own image, after our likeness ... So, God created man in his own image, in the image of God created he him; male and female created he them."**

"In OUR image!" It wasn't just a question of translation. These verses explained the meaning of Elohim. God is an image that combines the Divine Masculine and the Divine Feminine, and humanity reflects this image. How had I never noticed this? How did no one from the Church of my youth see this–after all, they picked the Bible apart over far less important issues. It troubled me that the early Church had marginalized the Goddess. It made me feel angry and sad, and I couldn't understand why this had happened.

I tried to make sense of it all. I began to consider that the Holy Spirit was a topic that most ministers avoided. Perhaps it was because She represented the Goddess, and the Holy Spirit was not male! Looking back now, I can see it clearly, but at the time, no one wanted to hear my questions, much less answer them.

When I read the Gnostic Gospel of Thomas: *"The Kingdom of God is inside you and all around you… not in a building of wood and stone."* The epiphany hit me like a ton of bricks! I was overthinking everything: "God" is not confined to a Church building and doesn't belong to any single denomination. Elohim, the Gods and Goddesses, could not be contained and could be called into a Wiccan Circle!

Since then, I have tried to make a safe place for Christopagans, Christian Witches, and Trinitarian Wiccans on many online platforms. I realized how important it was for like-minded individuals to have a place to share their thoughts and experiences. However, I wanted to advance my own knowledge of the Craft. I knew Trinitarian Wicca couldn't grow if I didn't progress personally.

So, I decided to try a new approach: Catechism classes. It was a way to fill in the gaps between what I knew about Protestant beliefs and what I understood about the modern Catholic tradition. Unfortunately, the original version of the book had been published for seven years, and my disapproval of the Church's origins and their removal of the Goddess had reached more people than I had anticipated. To my surprise and disappointment, I was denied admission to Catechism classes in my hometown.

My studies in Wicca were furthered by a local Priestess-turned-solitaire in my area. She was terrific and had endless patience with me, but I wanted to continue my studies in British Traditional Wicca. There were no Alexandrian covens anywhere near me. The closest formal coven was about two and a half hours away, but I was willing to make the drive weekly or as needed.

Excitedly, I applied for an in-person interview with two coven members but received a rejection letter shortly after. Not understanding why my application had been turned down, I decided to give them a call.

Once on the phone, they began ridiculing me for my book. I stated that I wanted to further my education in the Craft, but they accused me of trying to steal their coven's secrets. The conversation was humiliating. When I hung up the phone, I felt empty and defeated. I had been denied Catechism classes and now formal coven training. I didn't know what to do next.

In 2018, I moved back home with my mother, who was familiar with my book and additional manuscripts. Mom had grown up in a farming community that practiced many "old ways" at church, school, and with her younger family members. I was envious when she would read through the rituals I had written and would say, "Oh, we used to do that!" She encouraged me to return to my writing for additional books, meet new individuals, go to open Circles, and practice my faith.

Then, the Covid-19 pandemic hit, and the world sheltered in place. Christopagan author Kasey Hill and I attempted to revise the original book. Still, we were both unsatisfied with the outcome and pulled it from the market.

In September 2021, my mother passed away. For the next two years, I lived alone in her house, which had been my home for 38 years, surrounded by her essence and childhood memories. During this time alone, I thought about everything, with bad days and good days. Reflection is equally cruel and enlightening. Ultimately, I began to focus on what my Mom had encouraged me to do – develop my new ideas and finish my work. My Dad always told me, "Plan your work and work your plan."

I have since relocated and resumed my research with a new perspective. My confusion has been replaced by confidence. My doubts have been replaced by certainty. I took my parents' advice and have planned the Christopagan Series for Trinitarian Wiccans and Christian Witches.

While this book's title is similar, it addresses the same issues as the original but with twenty years of experience and further research. It's a new creature, written with love and clarity of direction. I'm excited about the new manuscripts in this series, but first, I needed to find closure with everything I didn't like about the first book, and… you are reading that now!

Piscean to Aquarian Shifts

"...there shall a man meet you, bearing a
pitcher of water; follow him into the house
where he entereth in." Luke 22:10.

Humanity is transitioning from the Piscean Age to the Age of Aquarius. The Piscean Age was the age of faith, relying on doctrine and dogmas handed down for thousands of years without question or challenge. The Aquarian Age is one of knowing. As we stand on this cusp, the vibrations of the shift are undeniable, and we are transitioning with it.

As I continue my studies and look around at the news in my community, our country, and the world, I'm beginning to understand the significance of these ages. The Piscean Age was known for its religious focus, and the Aquarian Age emphasizes a spiritual connection and understanding of the world around us. This shift has occurred over the past several decades; it will continue to usher in an era of global consciousness and compassion.

This new age calls us to embrace our individuality while celebrating our commonalities. We must learn to appreciate diversity, be mindful of our actions, recognize our interconnectedness with all life on Earth, and take responsibility for creating a better world. In other words, we must strive for peace within ourselves and among all cultures and nations.

This shift has been accompanied by a rise in spiritual awareness. This new age will be marked by increased understanding, connection to the Divine, and shared knowledge. As we move forward, we must recognize our unique paths and find solace in being present within ourselves.

In these changing times, many feel disconnected from the Universal Source, craving an increased link between themselves and their Higher Selves or the Deities they venerate. Opening yourself up to spiritual guidance can help you access deeper levels of wisdom that can help provide clarity when making life decisions or inspire creativity.

The Great Ages are determined by the Equinoxes' Precession, the 2150-year cyclic period that it takes the Sun to pass through each of the twelve stellar constellations associated with the zodiac. It is calculated based on the first day of Spring, the Vernal Equinox. When the astrology principles were assembled, the first day of Spring fell in the constellation of Aries. During the time of the Biblical Jesus, the first day of Spring was in Pisces.

The Piscean Age is believed to have begun around 200 ACE, and its correlations with Jesus are evident. Fish and water symbols appear frequently around him—for example, there is the Ichthus Fish, which

25

displays the first letters of the Greek word ICHTHUS, which means *fish*, and the phrase translates to *"Jesus Christ, Son of God, Savior."* The Solar Lord requests His disciples to be "fishers of men." The New Testament speaks of occasions involving fish and water: teaching an individual to fish so they may sustain themselves, feeding the multitude with five loaves and two fishes, and walking on water. Lastly, Jesus emphasized symbolic rebirth through a baptism of water and spirit.

When the sun rises in Aquarius, the Age of spiritual enlightenment begins. This period is associated with mystical understanding, heightened consciousness, and a potential for global peace. People become more aware that life is changing, although they may not comprehend why or how they can sense it in their daily routines. Concealed information surfaces, secrets are revealed, and religious cosmology starts to recede, shift, and reconfigure. Those who have always questioned religion can now reconcile their thoughts and emotions.

Naturally, this feeling unsettles those who resist change. The Aquarian energies instill a sense of peaceful liberation for many and a disquieting trepidation for others. The perception of Divinity is also experiencing a metamorphosis.

The Age of Aquarius represents a fundamental evolution in how humanity views itself. We are moving away from an individual emphasis on "me" and towards an appreciation for the collective "we." This shift is predicted to introduce new paradigms for how people can coexist peacefully with one another in balance and harmony.

Divinity is not confined by gender, race, or other earthly boundaries. The Great Abstract exists beyond our limitations yet is the all-encompassing force that binds us together. Deity is increasingly interpreted in terms that reflect ancient traditions while incorporating modern thought and experience. We are embracing concepts of the duality of a Father God and Mother God or male/female energies rather than seeing them as mutually exclusive.

People are recognizing that God transcends gender and comes in various forms, depending upon one's individual experience and beliefs. By removing limits placed upon our interpretation of Divinity, we open ourselves up to a broader understanding, which allows us to find comfort within our own version of faith while honoring what works for others.

Joachim de Fiore, a 12th-century monk, proposed that the precession of the ages was divided into three distinct Great Ages he associated with the Father, Son, and Holy Spirit. The first age is the Father's Age, encompassing the Old Testament, Creation Mythos, Giving of the Law, and Prophets. The second is Jesus' New Testament Age of the Son, characterized by his birth, death, resurrection, and the initial Church assembly. Lastly, there is the Age of the Holy Spirit, which pertains to the Church's diminishing role and increased spiritual piety without scriptures.

Gnostic philosopher Samual Aun Weor suggested that on February 4th, 1962, we crossed over into an Age of Aquarius where technology helped bring about knowledge and awareness. This new era reclaimed Goddess energy lost in the Piscean Age.

We can feel the cosmic shifts in our lives but often are uncomfortable admitting it. As we grow older, we acquire knowledge and experience, but reconciling these two aspects of ourselves can be difficult. People naturally seek greater wisdom to help them make sense of their lives and spiritual journeys.

The Age of Aquarius brings a new paradigm of understanding that challenges traditional beliefs regarding spirituality, faith, and divine intervention. As humanity evolves, many question the place for organized religion and look instead towards a more holistic approach to understanding the spiritual realm. The shift from dogmatic rules to a greater focus on intuition and inner exploration is multiplying, creating an environment where spiritual growth is possible and highly encouraged.

As this age progresses and knowledge expands, it has become easier to access information about metaphysical concepts such as reincarnation, astrology, occult teachings, and more. These topics were once considered taboo or that only spiritual gurus could safely explore without judgment or ridicule; however, now they are openly discussed by those seeking answers to life's mysteries.

This newfound openness brings an opportunity for people to reexamine their beliefs about spirituality without feeling judged or condemned by others. This is essential to growing into the Age of Aquarius, embracing our diverse perspectives on spiritual matters so that humanity can evolve into a higher state of consciousness.

History, science, and religion are often contradictory. However, it doesn't have to be that way if an individual does not consciously put them in opposition. Those with fundamentalist beliefs may assert that the Earth is 10,000 years old, while scientists point out that it's 4.54 billion years old. The existence of dinosaurs has already been proven by fossils; therefore, beliefs about the universe's timeline don't really matter.

Once, people believed that our planet was flat; now, its curved shape can be seen from low earth orbit. People are driven to explore and ask challenging questions. As mature individuals, we can forget this inclination for self-improvement occasionally. Still, children remind us through their inquisitive "why?" stage, questioning without any ill-intent. We cannot simply accept everything at face value anymore. The Age of Aquarius is causing us to ask big questions.

As the Age of Aquarius dawns, people start noticing unique, repeating patterns that can't be ignored. A popular example is the 11:11 phenomenon, often seen on a clock, calendar, street signs, or addresses. This sign indicates synchronicity and the universe's way of showing your true purpose. It can also signify angelic presence, spiritual awakening, or a Divine intervention.

According to numerology, 11 is a powerful number that represents intuition, inspiration, and transformation. Seeing 11:11 might suggest that you are on the right path and should take note of your thoughts and feelings. For some, this message holds an immense power that raises their consciousness to a higher level. Others dismiss 11:11 as nothing more than a coincidence. Both sides may be right since life has its own system of checks and balances to keep things in harmony, which is for the best! Otherwise, every little thing would send us into chaos!

The Age of Aquarius encourages us to challenge long-accepted norms regarding faith and explore unfamiliar concepts with curiosity rather than skepticism or fear. It is a time when individuals can express themselves more freely while striving for understanding rather than perfection. As we move further into this Age of Aquarius, it will be interesting to see what additions to the Christopagan landscape emerge that may reshape our understanding of God/dess worship. Regardless, one thing is sure: The Divine Feminine will continue to be an integral part of spiritual practice now and into the future!

Christopaganism
The Alchemy of Spiritual Paths

Christopaganism is an individualized spiritual practice that seeks to create a balance between Christianity and Paganism. Proponents of this belief system may consider Jesus the embodiment of the Divine Masculine and Feminine. Others may see Jesus as an ascended master or the equivalent of an adapted Pagan God. Others may view Jesus as a catalyst for enlightenment, regardless of whether it is historical, mythical, or metaphorical.

This path encourages direct connection with the divine rather than relying solely on religious texts or external authorities. Blending elements of both traditions create a unique third path with many interpretations and expressions. This allows for a diverse and inclusive spiritual practice.

The Christopagan community is experiencing a period of growth as those with various backgrounds and beliefs seek a more holistic spiritual path, bridging the gap between Christianity and Paganism. Christopaganism has become increasingly visible in both Christian and Pagan circles. This visibility has increased awareness of the many similarities between these two practices, leading to a growing acceptance of spiritual diversity.

Comparative studies become less critical between Christianity and Paganism as Christopagans focus on what unites them rather than what divides them, emphasizing the importance of personal experience over religious texts or external authorities.

Ultimately, Christopaganism is about finding your own path and journey toward enlightenment through the exploration of both Christianity and Paganism. This practice offers an opportunity to explore ancient techniques and modern adaptations to develop new methods for deepening one's connection with the Divine.

The Christopagan subculture has produced countless groups: Christian Wiccans, Trinitarian Wiccans, ChristoWiccans, Goddess Christians, Eco-Christians, Green Christians, Kabbalistic Wiccans,

Gnostic Christians, Gnostic Wiccans, Grail Priests, WicCatholics, EpiscoPagans, Pagans for Jesus, JeWitches, and Christian Witches. Likewise, many individuals have one foot in each world but choose not to label themselves.

Christopaganism is not necessarily accepted by its component faiths: Paganism and Christianity. Trinitarian Wicca holds beliefs that are considered blasphemous to some and disrespectful to others. One person's sacredness may be viewed as an abomination by another.

It is important to remember that "orthodoxy" is derived from the Greek ὀρθοδοξία, meaning the "correct opinion" or the "right belief." At the same time, "heresy" originates from αἵρεσις, translating to "a choice" or "thing chosen." This has been a problem for centuries, and most believe what they deem as the correct opinion is the right choice.

In the 2000s, books exploring various combinations of Christianity and Paganism were as controversial to both spiritual belief systems as Scott Cunningham's *Wicca: A Guide for the Solitary Practitioner* was in 1985's coven-trained Wiccan traditions. Change is always tricky, no matter how open-minded and liberal we like to believe ourselves to be. It is not unlike the growing pains the Protestant Reformation caused or when the Church of England pulled away from the Vatican's far-reaching arm.

Christopaganism is a prominent example of syncretic spiritual traditions. Syncretism is not a flash-in-the-pan. These movements have evolved throughout history in numerous cultures, allowing us to bridge spiritual differences.

This statement on syncretic religions by the late author and liturgist Issac Bonewits intrigues me. Many of you may identify with some of his comments and disagree with others. He explains:

> *"MesoPaganism" or "Meso-Paganism" is a general term for a variety of movements, both organized and nonorganized, started as attempts to recreate, revive, or continue what their founders thought were the best aspects of the Paleopagan ways of their ancestors (or predecessors), but which were heavily influenced*

(accidentally, deliberately and/or involuntarily) by concepts and practices from the monotheistic, dualistic, or nontheistic worldviews of Zoroastrianism, Judaism, Christianity, Islam, or early Buddhism.

Examples of MesoPagan belief systems would include Freemasonry, Rosicrucianism, Theosophy, Spiritualism, etc., as well as those forms of Druidism influenced by those movements, the many Afro-Diaspora faiths (such as Vodou, Santeria, Candomble, etc.), Sikhism, several sects of Hinduism that have been influenced by Islam and Christianity, Mahayana Buddhism, Aleister Crowley's religion/philosophy of Thelema, Odinism (some Norse Paganism), most "Family Traditions" of Witchcraft (those that aren't completely fake), and most orthodox (aka "British Traditionalist") denominations of Wicca.

Also included as Mesopagans would be the so-called "Christo-Pagans," those who call themselves "monotheist Pagans," and perhaps those Satanists who worship the Egyptian deity Set, if there really are any. The Satanists who insist that they don't worship anything other than themselves but who like to use the name Satan because it's "scary" are simply Christian heretics, along with the Secular Humanists and other Western atheists, because the God and Devil they don't believe in are the ones defined by Christian doctrine. Some MesoPagan belief systems may be racist, sexist, homophobic, etc. There are at least a billion Mesopagans living and worshiping their deities today."

I flinch at Bonewits' reference to 'so-called Christo-Pagans' after listing other syncretic paths he finds credible. However, I have never heard anyone in the Christopagan community refer to themselves as a "monotheist Pagan." If viewed from this perspective, Trinitarian Wiccans and most ChristoPagans could be considered polytheistic Christians. However, a monotheistic Pagan is usually regarded as henotheistic or practicing a form of monolatry.

Many authors have painted a primitive image of Paleopaganism, or pre-Christian paganism. But this view is limited and unhealthy. The reality is that Paleopagans built the Seven Wonders of the Ancient World, from the Greeks, who produced great philosophers, to the Egyptians, who created the Pyramids of Giza. These ancient societies were not only filled with hunter-gatherers celebrating fertility rituals for their crops; there was far more depth to pre-Christian culture than Neo-Paganism reflects.

In the pre-Christian era of Greece, three primary forms of paganism were practiced. The first was an agricultural type connected to shamanistic mysticism, usually found in areas outside of cities. The second was a political form of paganism that paid homage to powerful gods on Mount Olympus. The third and most intriguing form is frequently associated with today's secret societies because their initiation rituals have similar components to the Mysteries of Dionysus or The Eleusinian Mysteries.

This style of paganism was meant for a select few, namely the powerful and wealthy. This clandestine form of mysticism was shrouded in silence, but we know it influenced philosophers, sculptors, and artists. After the rise of Christianity, much information about these Greek mystery schools was lost.

Alchemy is a spiritual philosophy and a proto-science dedicated to self-transformation. The Alchemical process unites two substances commonly perceived as incompatible: Spirit and Matter. The Sun and the Moon, Sol and Luna, represent the opposing forces. They are also known as the Red King and the White Queen, respectively, representing the male and female.

The Union of the dissenting halves produces the Great Work, and the result of this combination is an offspring called the Rebis or the Great Child. The Rebis is the reconciliation of these opposing parental aspects, manifesting as a being of masculine and feminine characteristics. The Great Work is both the transformation process and the goal.

Christopaganism manifests as an example of alchemy in action. Christianity and Wicca are two principles that many perceive as incompatible, existing at opposite ends of the spiritual spectrum. Christianity is the Sun's masculine spiritual path; Wicca is the feminine path of the Moon; Christopaganism is the Rebis, the Great Child, possessing both male and female characteristics.

Christopagans seek to combine these two religions into something new, drawing from each to create a unique expression of spirituality that synthesizes elements from both traditions. Christopaganism strives to create a balanced approach to worship that blends tradition with contemporary values by uniting masculine and feminine energies through faith and practice.

The term *"Christopagan"* has recently become more widely accepted due to increased knowledge surrounding syncretic practices. As more individuals become aware of eclectic belief systems, acceptance will hopefully continue to grow, promoting union over separation.

Christopaganism is a syncretic path. Individually, Christianity and Wicca are also defined as syncretic paths. In their earliest incarnations, both gathered components from various co-existing cultures. The two spiritual halves meld in the heated crucible of gnosis.

The alchemical process is mutually devouring; each element consumes, absorbs, and transmutes the other until only the purest qualities remain. The crucible is the heat of gnosis. The Spirit Fire or Flame of Gnosis is the Holy Spirit of Christianity and the Goddess of Paganism.

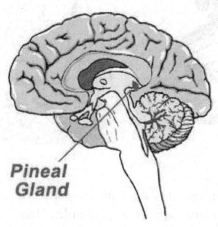

Pineal Gland

This flame burns away the calcination of the pineal gland, also referred to as the All-Seeing Eye or the Third Eye; it is centered between the brain's two hemispheres. Once the pineal gland is cleared of calcination, the Third Eye is no longer blind, allowing the initiate to see the Union's commonalities. The Union is the result, a third substance or ideology that did not previously exist. Thus, the Great Work is the spiritual goal and the journey to achieve it.

The ability or inability to accept the union or reunion is why this path is not for everyone. All forms of Christopaganism are a matter of perspective, and the various practices are matters of discernment. It depends on the individual's ability or willingness to accept Christianity and Paganism as interconnected.

Kabbalah and Gnosticism

"Be a lamp to yourself.
Be your own confidence. Hold to the truth
within yourself, as to the only Truth."
— Buddha

Trinitarian Wiccans can find the Goddess by studying the Kabbalah and Gnostic Gospels, two active mysticisms during the first three centuries before Orthodox Christianity began its development. These traditions pre-date the marginalization of the Great Mother.

Like Wicca, Gnostics and Kabbalists recognize a Goddess and a God, but also an origin and an offspring. The Divine Male and Female are understood as separate but equal manifestations of The All. Kabbalists recognize Yahweh as the Divine Masculine and Shekinah as the Divine Feminine, stemming from the genderless Supreme Being, Eheieh.

The Gnostics regarded Sophia as a Goddess emanating from the Good Father and the consort of the Logos. Many sects with radically conflicting views co-existed in Paleo-Christianity, referring to the historical era of the religion until the First Council of Nicaea in 325. Among them were:

- The Ebionites were a Jewish sect that practiced a strict form of Early Christianity, rejecting the divinity and resurrection of Jesus, believing he was a human prophet and the Jewish Messiah born naturally to Joseph and Mary. They denied the Original Sin and strictly adhered to Jewish law, observing the Sabbath, circumcision, and dietary restrictions. They believed these practices were necessary for salvation. Rejecting the Apostle Paul's teachings, they considered him an apostate who distorted the true message of Jesus and undermined the importance of Jewish law. The Ebionites had their own version of the Gospel of Matthew, known as the Gospel of the Ebionites, written in Hebrew or Aramaic. It emphasized the Jewishness of Jesus and contained teachings that aligned with their beliefs.

- The Essenes were a mystical Jewish sect that flourished during the Second Temple period from the 2nd century BCE to the 1st century CE. This sect was known for its strict interpretation of Jewish law and secluded communal living near bodies of water, believing in physical and spiritual purity by engaging in frequent ritual baths. The most famous community was near the Dead Sea, where the Dead Sea Scrolls were discovered. They practiced asceticism, abstaining from worldly pleasures and material possessions, and living simply with self-discipline. The Essenes were apocalyptic, believing the coming of a future Messiah was at hand and would bring about a new era of righteousness and justice for the Jewish diaspora. Their communities had a hierarchical structure for members progressing through different levels of initiation.

- The Simonians were an early Gnostic sect that emerged in the 1st century AD based on Simon Magus, an individual mentioned in the New Testament who claimed to possess great spiritual power. Simonians believed Simon Magus was a Divine incarnation of God, having otherworldly knowledge and performing miracles like Jesus. This sect viewed the world as inherently evil due to a flawed creation. They believed God was a transcendent and unknowable entity and that salvation could be attained through gnosis, which Simon Magus claimed to possess. The Simonians incorporated elements of Christianity, Judaism, and Hellenistic philosophy, blended with their unique interpretations. This sect practiced ritual magic and forms of sorcery that included incantations, sigils, and amulets. The Simonians faced opposition from early Church leaders, including the Apostles Peter and Paul, who condemned Simon Magus as a false prophet.

- The Montanists were a second-century Christian movement founded by Montanus, a Phrygian prophet from Asia Minor who claimed to have prophetic revelations from God that superseded scripture. They advocated for spiritual rigor, celibacy, asceticism, and ecstatic prophecy. They believed Montanus was divinely inspired and received direct revelations from the Holy Spirit. They emphasized the imminent return of Christ and the need for strict moral discipline in preparation for the end times. They believed that the Holy Spirit's revelations through Montanus were a sign of the final outpouring of the Spirit before the Second Coming. This movement was popular with both men and women, with prominent female leaders, Priscilla and Maximilla.

- The Marcionites were a small but influential group in the 2ⁿᵈ century, led by Marcion of Sinope, that challenged the still-forming Orthodoxy. Marcionites believed in a radical dualism, distinguishing between the God of the Old Testament as a lesser deity, the Demiurge, and the New Testament deity as the true God of love and mercy. This sect rejected the Hebrew Bible and the Mosaic Law, considering both incompatible with the teachings of Jesus. Instead, they embraced a modified version of the Gospel of Luke and ten of Paul's epistles. They rejected the idea of salvation through Jewish law and could only be gained through faith, prayer, and forgiveness. Marcionites claimed Jesus' body was spiritual, only appearing to be physical, rejecting physical incarnation, birth, and resurrection. They were known for their ascetic practices, advocating minimalism and detachment from worldly possessions. Marcion argued for a total separation between Judaism and Christianity, claiming Paul was the one true apostle sent by Jesus.

Kabbalah

Kabbalah is a Jewish form of mysticism that includes hermeticism, philosophy, and numerology. It literally means "that which is received," referencing the sacred knowledge and keys to enlightenment obtained directly from the Divine. By studying the iconic glyph of the Tree of Life, one can achieve spiritual perfection in this world and transcend time and space.

The Tree of Life appears in the Biblical story from Genesis, in which Adam and Eve are tested with a moral judgment in the Garden of Eden. God instructs Adam which trees to eat from and which to avoid. The Tree of Life is mentioned in Genesis 2:9 along with the Tree of Knowledge of Good and Evil, again in 2:15-17 KJV:

> *And out of the ground made the Lord God to grow every tree that is pleasant to the sight, and good for food; the tree of life also in the midst of the garden, and the tree of knowledge of good and evil.*
>
> *And the Lord God took the man, and put him into the garden of Eden to dress it and to keep it. And the Lord God commanded the man, saying, Of every tree of the garden thou mayest freely eat: But of the tree of the knowledge of good and evil, thou shalt not eat of it: for in the day that thou eatest thereof thou shalt surely die.*

From a Kabbalistic perspective, this is a limited view, omitting the importance of a representation of creation and the very existence of God. While Kabbalah primarily focuses on the Tree of Life, it indirectly addresses the Tree of Knowledge of Good and Evil through its teachings on the nature of the soul, the process of spiritual ascent, and the pursuit of balance between opposing forces.

Kabbalah teaches that a soul is composed of spiritual and earthly components. The spiritual aspect, associated with the Tree of Life,

40

symbolizes humanity's connection with Divinity. In contrast, the physical aspect links to the Tree of Knowledge and is connected to human experience and understanding of morality.

Followers of Kabbalah strive for spiritual improvement by ascending the sephirah or spheres on the Tree of Life. During this journey, the complexities of judgment posed by the Tree of Knowledge should be carefully examined since this will allow us to better understand our spirituality.

A central component in Kabbalah is reconciling opposing forces such as light and darkness, good and evil. Understanding the duality in human nature through engaging with the challenges presented in the Tree of Knowledge is also essential. Recognizing these concepts allows us to make conscious decisions that align and fortify our spiritual development.

Adam, Moses, and Abraham were all integral in protecting and propagating the tradition. According to legend, Adam was first gifted with this sacred knowledge from Archangel Raziel. However, he misused it and was expelled from the Garden of Eden. Later, Abraham was presented with Kabbalistic knowledge, only to lose it again. It was recovered when Moses ascended Mount Sinai twice, once to receive the Ten Commandments and a second time to receive the outer and inner teachings of Kabbalah.

The Kabbalah is a system of mystical thought that speaks to every person in its own way. Like an onion, it's made up of multiple layers. Peeling back one layer of understanding only reveals more layers of untouched spiritual concepts. Some students of the Tree of Life take their studies of Kabbalah too far, to the point where it becomes an obsession. While others cannot get a conceptual foothold on the information and never have the chance to delve into the many layers of Divine philosophy.

The Tree of Life is comprised of ten visible spheres and one invisible, representing the ten different emanations of the One. The ten spheres are arranged into three columns called the Three Pillars: the black pillar (feminine/negative), the gold pillar (masculine/feminine/balance), and the white pillar (masculine/positive).

The ten spheres are connected by twenty-two paths. These twenty-two paths correspond with the twenty-two letters of the Hebrew alphabet, all consonants. Each letter corresponds to a color, tone, direction, zodiac sign, and element. This is part of Paul Foster Case's writings for the Builders of the Adytum.

The glyph is divided into four worlds, each representing an aspect of reality. Atziluth is the world of emanation, a spiritual realm containing the spheres Kether, Chockmah, and Binah. Briah is the world of creation, an intellectual realm containing the spheres of Chesed, Geburah, and Tiphereth. Netzach, Hod, and Yesod form the emotional world of Yetzirah. Lastly, Malkuth is the only sphere in Assiah, the physical realm.

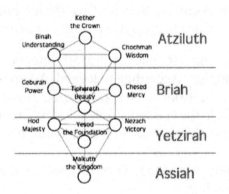

The Supernal Triad is a crucial part of the Tree of Life and consists of three sephiroth: Kether, Chokmah, and Binah. This Trinity forms the entrance to superior spiritual destinations. Kether signifies the oneness and origin of everything that exists. Chokmah embodies creative force and enlightenment, while Binah represents receptivity, intuition, and the power of perception.

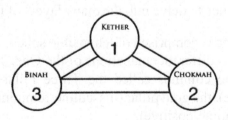

When Binah and Chokmah's energies meet, the Supernal Father and Mother's thoughts manifest in action. Their combined energies are channeled through Da'ath, the invisible pseudo-sphere that breaks the Tree of Life, separating the Supernal Triad of spheres in the Spiritual world from the lower spheres of the material world. Despite its profound symbolism, this invisible sphere doesn't have a number of its own. Patriarchal interpretations of this sphere signify humanity's fall from grace. However, Da'ath is a Hebrew word translated to knowledge. It is the point on the Tree where all the spheres converge as one, creating a reflective mirror effect.

Da'ath can be accessed by uniting the Wisdom of Chokmah with the Understanding of Binah. Then, we can look inward and ask ourselves if we are in good graces with the Divine and what can be done to amend it if we are not. Without being in touch with our inner deity, we cannot activate the Godspark within.

The First Sphere at the top of the Tree of Life is Kether, the Crown of the Tree of Life. This sephirah is a gateway to an unfamiliar and infinite realm with no fixed form. In Kabbalistic philosophy, humans can't understand Kether's true nature. To reflect on this concept in our lives, we ask ourselves: *How close am I to being a positive reflection of God?* Though it may be an unachievable goal, it is still any spiritual seeker's aim. The corresponding God-name for this sphere is Eheieh.

The Second Sphere on the white pillar is Chokmah, the sphere of Wisdom. Kabbalists acknowledge this sphere as the Supernal Father. The lesson of this sphere is to continue to seek mystical Wisdom. One can also ask, *How can I best use my Wisdom? Am I using my God-like Wisdom in a positive, reflective manner?* While humanity cannot fully grasp the Wisdom of the Creator, this Wisdom is meant for us to strive to be more like the Divine. The corresponding God-name for this sphere is YHWH or Yahweh/Jehovah.

The Third Sphere resting on the black pillar is Binah, the sphere of Understanding. Binah is acknowledged as the Great Mother, situated at the top of the female column, housing an abundance of energy that keeps our chakras in motion. To apply this lesson, we must ask ourselves: *How large is my capacity for Understanding? Have I adequately processed the Wisdom obtained from Chokmah, or do I need more time to comprehend it? How can I use the Wisdom of the Chokmah with the Understanding of Binah?* The corresponding God-name for this sphere is Elohim.

The seven remaining spheres on the Tree of Life comprise the material world: mental, emotional, and physical. These spheres are reflections of our humanity, embodying the characteristics of the Divine and, subsequently, society. Likewise, they interact with each other, each having a distinct role in our lives.

The Fourth Sphere, Chesed, resides on the white pillar and represents Mercy. It is commonly understood to reflect love, compassion, and empathy. The Hebrew God-name affiliated with this sphere is El. Manly P. Hall humorously refers to "El" as the Divine article. It also appears as a suffix -el in the word angel, which signifies "the shining ones." This sphere emphasizes God the Father's role as a provider for all humanity.

The Fifth sphere rests on the black pillar is Geburah, symbolizing Strength, Fear, and Severity. It promotes self-control to achieve aspirations or uphold standards and carries the appellation Elohim Gibor. This sphere focuses on remedying faults instead of inflicting judgment, penalty, or revenge, ultimately bringing conditions back in line with Divine law as practically as possible.

The Sixth Sphere of Tiphereth is located on the Middle Pillar, or Gold Pillar, symbolizing Beauty and Balance. It has masculine and feminine traits and represents a graceful integration of creative energy and realistic problem-solving. Eloah va Da'ath is the God-name connected to this sphere; it translates to 'Goddess of Knowledge' in English. The genderless nature of this sphere on the Tree of Life alludes to Jesus' male-female balance. Tiphereth serves as the Promised Child of Binah and Chokmah levels. However, its mysterious invisible sphere, Da'ath, also corresponds to Jesus, the embodiment of divine Wisdom and Understanding. Moreover, its Sun (Son) relationship further emphasizes the principle of the Divine Child.

The Seventh Sphere, Hod, sits at the bottom of the Black Pillar. It represents feminine aspects and stands for Glory and Honor. Additionally, it is known as the emotional sphere associated with logic and rationality, as well as an individual's ability to reason. Elohim Sabaoth is the God-Name connected with this sphere, which roughly translates to "the God-Goddesses of everyone."

The Eighth sphere, Netzach, is usually linked to Hod. It positions itself on the white pillar, representing male aspects such as Victory and Achievement. This sphere has ties to creative ideas, ambition, motivation, and willpower. The God-name connected with Netzach is YHWH Sabbaoth, which translates to "the God of Hosts." Together, they work harmoniously to bring Divine love and grace to all human souls.

The Ninth Sphere, Yesod, lies on the gold pillar, representing male and female characteristics. This sphere represents Foundation, and its connection to the divine is expressed in the God-name Shaddai el Chai, meaning "the Almighty Living God." The correspondences of this Sphere are closely linked with the moon, femininity, and life cycles such as menstruation, birth, and death. This sphere is one's starting point for path walking on the Tree of Life. Here, one begins to access their subconscious mind and understand intuition to become closer to the Divine.

The Tenth sphere is called Malkuth, meaning The Kingdom or Divine Presence on Earth. It has a strong connection with the God-name of Adonai, which means Lord, but also to the feminine figure of Shekinah. This link between the Divine Feminine and our planet gives this sphere numerous interpretations.

Beyond its spiritual significance, the Tree of Life also holds a remarkable mathematical harmony in fractals, Fibonacci sequences, and the golden ratio.

Fractal patterns throughout nature are integral to understanding how energy is exchanged within the Tree of Life. A fractal pattern is a repeating geometric pattern at different scales or sizes. The Tree of Life symbolizes this phenomenon, with each successive layer getting smaller and more detailed as it moves away from Kether, the top sphere. This principle also applies to the Fibonacci sequence, integer in a series in which each numeral equals the sum of the two preceding numbers: 0, 1,

1, 2, 3, 5, 8, 13, 21, etc. It can be seen in many aspects of nature, including tree branches, shells, flower petals, and spiral galaxies.

In addition to these mathematical patterns, another remarkable feature hidden within the structure of the Tree of Life is that it contains elements that demonstrate harmony through proportion, namely the golden ratio or Divine Proportion, which has aesthetically pleasing qualities when implemented into design work. This ratio is represented by a single number, 1.6180339887... to infinity, denoted by the Greek letter Phi (Φ).

The mathematical beauty of the Tree of Life demonstrates how breathtakingly intricate our universe truly is and serves as an example for us to strive for balance and harmony in our lives, internally between our mind, body, and spirit and externally between ourselves and Nature. All these patterns indicate orderliness with elegance, suggesting harmony among all things.

Due to the complex nature of the Kabbalah, Hebrew males were forbidden to study this mystical work until the age of 40. It was believed that studying the Kabbalah earlier in life would have severe mental repercussions. The vessel, which Kabbalists call the human body and receiving mind, is not mentally ready to comprehend the depth of the Tree of Life.

The number 40 has a special place in Kabbalah and the Torah. Forty is the numerical value of the Hebrew letter *mem,* which means water; this encompasses knowledge of God and is likened to water. Moses was said to have been in Heaven for 40 days to receive the Torah, and the Flood was said to have lasted for 40 days and 40 nights. Forty also corresponds to the 40 weeks from conception until the fetus is fully formed.

Forty represents all four sides of the world, each with ten spheres. In some cases, when someone's found guilty of a crime by a rabbinical court, they may get punished with symbolic "forty less one" lashes. This "forty less one" figure acts as a means of bringing about change and forgiveness. It's assumed that by age forty, we can grasp and comprehend our teacher's innermost intentions, which may have been previously obscured.

Gnosticism

The origins of Gnosticism are complex and can be cumbersome to decipher. The term "Gnosticism" comes from the Greek word "gnosis," meaning "knowledge." Gnostics believed receiving this special knowledge would lead to salvation and liberation from the material world.

Gnosticism emerged in the Hellenistic period, primarily in the eastern Mediterranean region, during the first few centuries CE. Some scholars argue that Gnosticism has roots in the Jewish mystical traditions of the Second Temple.

Foundational belief points for Gnosticism include:

Dualism: Gnostics believed in a fundamental duality between the material world, considered evil and created by a lesser, imperfect deity known as the "Demiurge," opposed to the spiritual world, which was good and created by the True "Good Father" God. They saw the material world as a prison they sought to escape.

Divine Spark: Gnostics believed that a Divine spark or "pneuma" (spirit) exists within every human being, originating from the realm of the true God. This Divine spark longs to be reunited with its divine source, and knowledge or gnosis is how this reunion is achieved.

Sophia and the Aeons: Gnostics believed in a series of spiritual beings or Aeons who emanated from the true God. One of these Aeons, Sophia, played a significant role in Gnostic cosmology. According to some Gnostic systems, Sophia fell from the divine realm, creating the material world and the flawed Demiurge.

Salvation through Knowledge: Gnostics emphasized the importance of acquiring secret knowledge or gnosis to liberate oneself from the material world. This knowledge involved understanding reality's true nature, the human soul's divine origin, and the meaning of Jesus' teachings.

Denial of Jesus' Humanity: Some Gnostics denied the true humanity of Jesus, believing that he only had the appearance of a physical body.

They saw Jesus as a divine being who came to impart knowledge to humankind rather than offer a physical sacrifice for sins.

Dualistic Morality: Gnostics often developed a dualistic moral framework, distinguishing between the spiritual and the material. They believed the material world was inherently evil, leading some to embrace ascetic practices and reject worldly pleasures.

Gnosticism was considered heretical by mainstream Christian authorities, and many Gnostic texts were suppressed and destroyed. Until the discovery of the Nag Hammadi Library in Egypt in 1945, including the *Gospel of Thomas*, the *Gospel of Philip*, and the *Secret Book of John*, our knowledge of Gnosticism was primarily due to its opponents, the early Christian theologians like Irenaeus and Hippolytus, who criticized Gnostic teachings.

Gnosticism was a polytheistic movement with a diverse collection of beliefs and practices. Each Gnostic group had its own unique cosmologies and mythologies. After the crucifixion and the resurrection of Jesus, there were many sects of early Christianity. This is very different from today's denominations in that the sects differed on the actual framework of Christianity, and modern denominations differ only from the point of view within a standard framework. The Councils of Nicaea I (325 A.C.E.), Constantinople I (381 A.C.E.), Ephesus (431 A.C.E.), and Chaldean (451 A.C.E.) determined this framework.

To sum up the problems of the Early Christians, one could say that there was nothing "organized" about these forms of religion. The sects of early Christianity often fought within themselves, but there was equal peaceful coexistence among the groups. Like modern Christians, each group professed to know "the single truth" concerning Jesus, salvation, and the source of the wrath of the Old Testament God. The Early Church councils decided the contents of the Bible, and the Gnostics lost.

The number of Gnostic sects is staggering. However, the Valentinians were the largest group, followed by the Sethians and the Basilideans. Each group professed to know "the single truth" concerning Jesus, salvation, and the source of the Old Testament God's wrath. A force of arms decided the contents of today's Bible; the Gnostics lost. Before the Nag Hammadi discovery, little had been known about Gnosticism's influence on early Christianity.

The views of the Gnostics were radically different; their approach to Christianity was mystical and eclectic. Salvation was a state of being achieved through philosophy and introspection, not adherence to doctrine and sacraments. Salvation was not an original Christian precept. They viewed this God as perfect and singular yet possessing a Goddess. They believed Jesus was the celestial offspring from the Union of God and Goddess, thus forming the Blessed Trinity.

The concept of the demiurge is another aspect that separated the Gnostics from the emerging Orthodoxy. The demiurge is not a name but a description the Gnostics gave to the Old Testament God, who was perceived as vengeful and cruel. The Gnostics did not believe he was the Good Father of Jesus' ministries.

The Gnostic's creation mythos varies significantly from the Hebrew Bible in the book of Genesis. Sophia is the active creative force, and Her consort, the Good Father, is the passive creative force. This myth states that Sophia desires a child but does not actively mate with the Good Father. Her thoughts were manifested by Her powerful will. Sophia's desire was veiled, casting a shadow of otherworldly matter that lacked Spirit. This imbalance created the imperfect deity known as the demiurge or Yaldabaoth. To the Gnostics, the demiurge was a poor reflection of the heavenly hosts.

Embarrassed by Her actions, Sophia banished the imperfect godform from the celestial realm and gave it an independent existence. She did not want the other Aeons, immortal beings, in Heaven to see Her mistake. Sophia then enters a cloud and begins to cry for all eternity at Her foolish error.

The Gnostics called the Old Testament deity Yaldabaoth, which means "child, pass through to here," or the name Samael, meaning the *"blind god"* or *"the God of the blind."* This type of blindness addresses the inability to recognize the spiritual Mysteries within us. This godform is the arrogant artisan deity of the Old Testament. In his arrogance, he spoke of no other Gods, not recognizing his mother, Sophia.

In Gnosticism, the demiurge was not the creator of the material world. He was an artisan, implying an entity that is a builder or re-shaper of the existing world. He is not considered Divinity but an archon, a lower order of spirits or aeons. According to the Gnostics, the demiurge could endow humans only with a psyche or sensuous soul; only the True God could add the pneuma, the rational soul. The Greek term pneuma is associated with the New Testament's Holy Spirit. The Gnostics identified the demiurge as Jehovah, the Israelite deity.

Some Gnostics taught that the world is ruled by evil archons, among them being the deity of the Old Testament, who held captive the spirit of humanity. They proposed the demiurge was Satan, the Hebrew *"ha-satan"* or adversary of the Good Father.

In the demiurge's arrogance and ignorance, He creates the visible world but begins to withhold knowledge from humanity. Adam and Eve were instructed not to eat from the Tree of Knowledge of Good and Evil. If they did eat, they would become self-aware, develop individuality, and formulate questions, ideas, and opinions. This sudden independence angers the Old Testament God, beginning His vengeful reign.

There are many creation stories worldwide, and this is not the only one among Gnostics. However, it does give insight into the difference between the vengeful Deity of the Old Testament, and the loving God Jesus proclaims in the New Testament.

From the Nag Hammadi Library, "The Gospel of The Egyptians" tells another creation myth that begins with a trinity: The Androgynous Father, The Virginal Mother Barbelo, and the Silent Son. From Barbelo, the feminine manifestation mentioned in the scriptures, rose four ogdoads, or lights, and their consorts.

The Gnostics also disagreed with the orthodoxy about who Jesus was and his real purpose on earth. The Gnostics did not believe the demiurge sent Jesus; instead, he was sent by the Good Father and the Great Mother. Jesus' purpose was to correct the demiurge's injustices against humanity, emphasizing personal gnosis over blanket orthodoxy.

The Gnostics believed that Jesus taught through the secrets of the Mysteries, which he did not impart to the masses. Gnosis is intimate knowledge that must be experienced, not gained through the clergy. This intuitive knowledge is imparted to each individual through introspection, meditation, and contemplation.

The Gnostics also disagreed that man was naturally sinful but thought this human error was due to spiritual ignorance. By gnosis, they proposed the world could correct its erring ways and gain salvation. The Gnostics deemed there were many "secret teachings" that followers could only receive directly from Jesus. Like the Kabbalists, these teachings were revealed once when one had made his/her vessel pure and clean to receive such enlightenment.

The Gnostics were the more literary of the early sects, as evidenced by the discovery of the Nag Hammadi scrolls. This collection contained previously unknown gospels by the other eight disciples, additional books of Acts of the Apostles as told from the other ten apostles, the apocalypses of Moses, the Virgin Mary, and the fragmented Gospel of Mary Magdalene. Additionally, there is the Infancy Gospel of Thomas, which relays the stories of the early life of Jesus, as well as the infancy of the Virgin Mary.

These scrolls proclaim a perfect God filled with enlightenment too vast to comprehend. They also speak of various Goddesses favored by the pre-Nicene Christian factions. Different Gnostic sects believed God was not a Divine Being from another realm but resided within each of us.

In retrospect, we can see the common underlying themes and similarities between these mystical belief systems, and this is the basis for applying the Blessed Trinity to Wicca. All three faiths believe meditation, inner contemplation, and ritualized connection are the preferred ways to commune with Deity. These paths' belief systems suggest that the oneness of humanity with the Divine cannot be understood by reading alone.

The Gnostics and the Kabbalists share similar spiritual enlightenment goals and share the theories of Divine knowledge by Divine revelation. They each sought the truth and the answers to the paradoxical religious questions of life. There are five essential questions addressed by the Kabbalists and the Gnostics:

1. Why does the world possess characteristics of both good and evil when the world was created by a God, who is all good?

2. Why does this world have limits when a God who knows no limits created it?

3. Why does humanity possess good and evil attributes if an all-loving God created humankind in his image?

4. Why does humanity have limits when created by a God who knows no limits?

5. If God is limitless, infinite, genderless, without form, all good, and all-knowing, how can humanity pretend to know God?

Wicca, Gnosticism, and Kabbalah are three mystical belief systems with underlying similarities. All three encourage the development of our natural psychic abilities for self-control and focusing our thoughts.

Discovering Your Inner Goddess

Trinitarian Wicca is based on the Elohian Pantheon, which consists of the Good Father and the Solar Lord Jesus, the Kabbalistic-Gnostic, or Elohian Goddesses from the first three centuries ACE, and cultural figures absorbed by Catholicism. As there's no official recognition of the Sacred Feminine in Church doctrine, people coming to this tradition often wonder, *"Who is the Goddess? What does she stand for? How do I find Her?"*

It is natural to enter this meditation with a specific Goddess in mind, and through this contemplative exercise, you will find confirmation of your intuitive feelings. Understanding that the Great Mother may reveal herself to you in various forms and speak to you through multiple voices is crucial. If this happens, take heart; these Goddesses are there to provide you with strength and guidance through their unique qualities.

The number nine is sacred to the Goddess, symbolizing the triple Goddess and the strength of three trinities. In numerology, the number 9 represents completion but not finality. It signifies succession and completion, indicating the end of one cycle and the beginning of a new one. The moon's monthly cycle lasts around 29.5 days; however, it takes nine months to complete its entire lunar cycle.

Nine is the last single-digit or cardinal number with the highest numerical value. The number nine has a unique property: when multiplied by any single-digit number, the sum of the digits of the product always equals nine. For example: $9 \times 2 = 18$, $1 + 8 = 9$; $9 \times 3 = 27$, $2 + 7 = 9$; $9 \times 4 = 36$, $3 + 6 = 9$; $9 \times 5 = 45$, $4 + 5 = 9$; $9 \times 6 = 54$, $5 + 4 = 9$; $9 \times 7 = 63$, $6 + 3 = 9$; $9 \times 8 = 72$, $7 + 2 = 9$; $9 \times 9 = 81$, $8 + 1 = 9$.

The number nine embodies Divine Feminine energy expressed as intuition, compassion, creativity, and nurturing. It adds to the Trinitarian Wiccan understanding of the Holy Spirit as the Goddess of the Blessed Trinity, noting Her nine gifts in Galatians 5:22-23: ***"But the fruit of the Spirit is love, joy, peace, longsuffering, gentleness, goodness, faith, Meekness, temperance: against such there is no law."***

Although the traditional notion of honoring the Goddess is commonly associated with female Wiccans, male Wiccans can also benefit from reconnecting to Her energy, understanding its importance in their spiritual practice. By connecting to the Divine Feminine, they can gain a greater appreciation for nature's beauty and wisdom, nurturing a deeper connection with the Earth.

Reclaiming the Goddess helps men honor their inner feminine if they embrace Her many benefits. Accepting the Divine Feminine allows them to express themselves authentically and put aside preconceived ideas about masculinity, providing a space free of judgment. By embodying both masculine and feminine energies, they can achieve a balance that is a source of inner strength.

Connecting to the Goddess also allows men to reflect on their relationships and interactions with others. This helps them identify patterns that may be holding them back from making meaningful connections, aiding in creating healthier relationships with family, friends, or partners.

Finally, reclaiming the Goddess gives male Wiccans access to qualities such as compassion, creativity, empathy, intuition, understanding, and vulnerability—all essential for living their true life. By connecting to the Divine Feminine within, male practitioners can tap into these qualities more readily and learn how to use them effectively in everyday situations.

Overall, cultivating a relationship with the Goddess provides male Wiccans access to powerful qualities crucial to establishing and maintaining balance in everyday life. Reclaiming this energy encourages self-discovery and appreciation for one's unique journey towards spiritual growth.

In this meditation, you will require nine candles of your choosing, each to represent a different Goddess. Safely arrange them on your altar, table, or floor in a position that allows you to sit comfortably. Plan to meditate for at least 45 minutes, dedicating at least 5 minutes to each Goddess candle. Envision a pentacle at the center of a cross, with four candles placed at the cardinal positions of the cross and five candles at the points of the pentacle.

To fully immerse yourself in this meditation, ensure you have privacy and can focus without the fear of interruptions. Set the atmosphere in the room by dimming the lights, eliminating unnecessary sounds, and silencing your cell phone. Light your preferred incense once distractions have been minimalized, and allow yourself to relax. Quiet your mind and center your energy.

Assign a specific Goddess to each candle, choosing from the Elohian pantheon, which includes the Holy Spirit, Shekinah, Brigid, Mother Mary, Sophia, Asherah, Anath, Lilith, Zoe, Guadalupe, and Mary Magdalene. Write the name of each Goddess on the side of the corresponding candle and anoint it with your favorite oil. Arrange the candles to form the nine points.

Begin by casting a circle and lighting each candle, invoking each Goddess as you go. Starting with the top candle, gently hover your hand over each flame. Speak aloud the name of each Goddess, focusing on what she symbolizes to you and addressing any concerns or questions you may have about her. Be as concise or detailed as you wish, but include the primary inquiries to help you become acquainted with each Goddess.

Allow yourself to visualize the Goddess floating slightly above the ground before you. Her body is translucent and radiates with an inner light; the power emanating from Her is majestic and welcoming. Her arms and legs move leisurely like the branches of a willow tree, yet with the strength of the mighty oak. Her long hair cascades over each shoulder as the first rays of dawn light up Her form. The Earth's gentle curve is reflected in the shape of Her breasts and belly as the Sun colors Her skin a golden shade.

Allow your senses to find Her glorious scent. Is it that of the sea, salty and crisp, or floral scents of roses, lilacs, and jasmine? Does She emit the darker grounding scents of sandalwood or patchouli? Allow the earthy aroma of the soil and forest to mingle with this scent until it lingers with you so that it can be recalled in the future.

Allow Her to speak to you with the voice of the wind, soft and moving, never harsh or sharp. Her words are rhythmic and melodic, not rushed but in perfect cadence. Each word She speaks is a pearl of Wisdom:

"Welcome, my child. I am the Goddess. I have been here since the beginning; I have come here to guide you and give you the strength to begin your mystical journal. Take a deep breath, relax, and find the calming center within. Believe in yourself and trust your instincts. Don't be afraid to take risks even if you think you might fail. Every risk is a chance for growth. Don't let any obstacles stand in your way. Remember why you started this journey. Believe in yourself, and remember, you all can make anything happen. I have faith in you; you have the potential to do great things."

Experiencing the Goddesses should be a peaceful but exhilarating experience. If you feel overwhelmed by Her celestial energies, take a deep breath, calm yourself, and remember this is a new spiritual experience. As you make room for the Great Mother in your life, it is natural for new emotions to surface. Remain open to any energy sensations that may arise, such as tingling, pressure, or inexplicable waves of euphoria.

Return your attention to your candles. One may captivate your focus more than the others. Observe the candles as they burn, each charged with the name and energy of an individual Goddess. Some will display unique behavior, burning faster than others or dancing to get your attention. Flames can burn extremely tall and quickly shorten, sometimes crackling and popping.

On the other hand, a candle representing a Goddess with a calm energy level may give the impression of being less responsive or act more slowly in its expression. This, too, is a form of connection. These subtle movements are significant, and the flames emote distinctly as the Goddess speaks directly to you.

Do not rush this ritual or pressure yourself to connect with a specific Goddess. If you seek the Goddess, she will reveal herself to you. After all, she has been with you since the very beginning.

Rite of Dedication

A dedication ritual is a precursor to initiation. This dedication ritual is a personal and individualized experience, where the practitioner declares their intention to follow the Wiccan path and align themselves with the principles and beliefs of Trinitarian Wicca. It is the next step on your journey. During the dedication ritual, the practitioner makes a promise to themselves, the Blessed Trinity, and the Wiccan community.

While coven initiation traditionally involves passing esoteric knowledge from one practitioner to another, the dedication ritual in Trinitarian Wicca focuses on the individual's personal commitment and spiritual transformation. As the number of solitary Wiccans grows and new traditions emerge, it is time to rethink this cherished Rite of Passage.

The dedication ritual is a significant step on the path of spiritual growth. This commitment is like giving birth to a new version of yourself, where you ascend to a higher plane of understanding. It's a tangible show of your devotion to learning, mystical occurrences in the Circle, and the internal metamorphosis that comes with it.

Composing a statement of your intent and spiritual pursuits is recommended. Stating your initial beliefs about the Craft, your views on the Blessed Trinity, and your goals for the following year. These vows should include commitments to personal growth, ethical behavior, and the pursuit of knowledge and profound wisdom.

Copy your dedication statement that reflects your inner desires into the first pages of your magickal journal. This serves as your starting point, displaying your initial beliefs and knowledge. After completing an entire cycle of festivals, you can look back at this entry to reflect on how far you have come and your original intent.

The ritual can be as simple as lighting one candle and reading your statement aloud. Or this ritual can be more elaborate if you prefer: casting a Circle, calling the quarters, invoking the Trinity. Adding candles, incense, and libations will enhance the setting for your dedication ritual.

> *On this day,___ day of __, 20__ I, [birth name], chose*
> *to dedicate myself to the Goddess, God, and Solar Lord;*
> *I will uphold the Wiccan Rede, celebrate the eight*
> *sabbats and the thirteen esbats. On this day/night, bless*
> *me as I begin my magical journey as [new magickal*
> *name]. So as I will it, So mote it be!*

Blow out the candle, and rest assured that you have officially taken the first step on your spiritual journey. It is the perfect time to start your magickal journal or Book of Shadows. Include the words of your dedication ritual and any candles, oils, or incense to personalize the ceremony. Include your thoughts and feelings at the time of your dedication. It will serve as a measure of your spiritual growth and be invaluable in the future.

The Sacred Altar

The Altar is at the center of Wiccan practice. It is our personal temple and sacred space, adorned with four essential tools, each signifying a powerful spiritual connection. Don't overtax yourself when assembling your altar—just let it come naturally. You will create a platform for your mystical relationship with the Blessed Trinity. In traditional and eclectic Wicca, the altar is binary, with the Goddess on the left side of the altar and the Divine Masculine on the right. Trinitarian Wiccans assemble an altar divided into three sections with a center area dedicated to Jesus the Solar Lord.

There are four primary tools on the Wiccan altar. Each instrument corresponds with one of the four cardinal directions, has a specific role to perform during a ritual, and holds symbolic knowledge revealed in the Mysteries, which you will learn as you progress on your spiritual journey. These tools are symbolic and serve as articles of focus; they are tools for meditation and visualization, triggering symbolic gnosis.

Athame: a ritual knife with a double-edged blade that represents the element of fire. It is not used for physical cutting but as a symbolic tool for directing energy. The athame is employed in casting circles, invoking deities, and consecrating objects. Its presence on the altar signifies the power of transformation and manifestations. It also represents the male aspect of the Divine in fertility rites.

Wand: a length of wood or metal that represents the element of air. It serves as a tool for directing energy, similar to the athame, but with a more subtle approach. Its presence on the altar signifies creativity, inspiration, and the power of the mind. The wand can be used to draw symbols in the air, invoke non-corporeal energies, and direct them.

Chalice: a stemmed cup or goblet of silver, glass, or earthenware embodies the element of water. It symbolizes the feminine aspect of divinity and the womb of creation. The chalice is used to hold sacred liquids, such as water or wine, which are consecrated and consumed during rituals. The chalice and its contents represent the flow of emotions, intuition, and nurturing aspects of the Goddess. By drinking from the chalice, Wiccans connect with the Great Mother and take Her life-giving energies into themselves. It also represents the female aspect of the Divine in fertility rites.

Pentacle: a round disk or plate of wood, wax, metal, or clay with a pentagram that embodies the element of earth. It represents the physical realm, stability, and grounding. The pentacle is used for consecrating objects, charging crystals, and invoking the energies of the earth. It symbolizes the interconnectedness and the balance between the spiritual and material worlds. By placing objects upon the pentacle, they are infused with sacred energy and aligned with their intentions.

It is essential for newcomers to the Craft to realize that these tools are not mere objects but sacred conduits that enable Wiccans to tap into the earth and cosmic energies to create a harmonious balance between the spiritual and physical realms.

Additional articles on the altar may include statues or figurines, image cards, and Novena candles as the visual representation of God, Goddess, and the Solar Lord. These focus articles are tools for meditation and visualization, triggering symbolic gnosis.

The best way to honor your ancestors is to place personal objects, a photo of a loved one, or perhaps a piece of jewelry belonging to a deceased family member. Amulets, charged crystals, tarot cards, or runes can enhance one's spiritual experience during the ceremony.

The practitioner's *Book of Shadows and Light* should be included on or near the altar. Some individuals may need to access their magickal journal for details and reminders during rituals, locating correspondences, or other references.

Incense is essential in any ritual because it is another form of cleansing the sacred area. It causes clinging negative energy to be banished from one's psyche, aura, or energy field. This negative energy may come home with you from work or the oppressive stress associated with daily life. The Israelites are among the many groups that used incense in their rituals, and the smoke carried prayers upward to the Divine.

The Trinity Candles can be white year-round except for Samhain, when black is more appropriate. Using seasonal colors at the sabbats can give variety. Trinitarian Wiccan set the altar facing east, solely corresponding to the rising sun and moon.

In Exodus 40:22-30, the God of the Old Testament instructs Moses to set up the Tabernacle to house the Ark of the Covenant using the elemental cardinal points. Moses was directed to set the table on the north side of the Tabernacle. Upon this table, Moses placed the bread, representing the element of earth, which we can interpret as being used for communion or Cakes and Ale.

In Exodus 40:24, Moses sets the candlestick, representing the element of fire, on the south side of the Tabernacle. Exodus 40:27, the Bible states that Moses burned sweet incense. In Exodus 40:29, the altar burned offerings, representing the element of air, placed at the entrance of the Tabernacle in the east. Lastly, in Exodus 40:30, the element of water is used in a basin in the west for washing hands and feet before entering.

Consecrating the Tools

Tools are essential components of ritual; they are symbols that are the keys to unlocking ancient Mysteries. Before using them, they should be cleansed to banish lingering energies, erase any metaphysical history, and, most importantly, create a reciprocating bond between the Deity and the wielder.

A simple but effective consecration ritual should be performed within a cast Circle. Begin by assembling your magickal tools – specifically the athame, wand, chalice, and pentacle within the circle.

Items Needed:
Container of water
Container of Salt
Stick/Cone Incense or Frankincense Resin on Coal
Candle

[Hold your hand over the container of water and say:]
I call upon the Blessed Trinity:
I ask you to bless this water for
the consecration of my tools,
Representing my Goddess of the Sea
So as I will it, So mote it be.

[Hold your hand over the container of salt and say:]
I call upon the Blessed Trinity:
I ask you to bless this salt
t for the consecration of my tools,
Representing my Goddess of the Earth
So as I will it, So mote it be.

[Hold your hand over the candle and say:]
I call upon the Blessed Trinity:
I ask you to bless this flame
for the consecration of my tools,
Representing my God of the Fire
So as I will it, So mote it be.

[Hold your hand over the incense and say:]
I call upon the Blessed Trinity:
I ask you to bless this incense
for the consecration of my tools,
Representing my God of the Air
So as I will it, So mote it be.

[Pass the athame, wand, chalice, or pentacle/cross
through the smoke of the incense and say:]
May the element of air instill intelligence,
Discernment, and logic,
I consecrate this [tool] with incense for
My magickal workings.
Imbued with love,
This [tool] is now a mystical storehouse
and a conduit of the Blessed Trinity.

[wave the tool safely over the flame of a candle and say:]
May the element of fire instill passion,
courage and logic,
I consecrate this [tool] over this flame for
My magickal workings.
Imbued with love,
This [tool] is now a mystical storehouse
and a conduit of the Blessed Trinity.

[sprinkle water lightly and say:]
May the element of water instill intuition,
clairvoyance and empathy,
I consecrate this [tool] with this water for
my magickal workings.
Imbued with love,
This [tool] is now a mystical storehouse
and a conduit of the Blessed Trinity.

[sprinkle salt lightly and say:]
May the element of earth instill balance,
solidarity and fortitude,
I consecrate this [tool] with this salt for
my magickal workings.
Imbued with my love,
This [tool] is now a mystical storehouse
and a conduit of the Blessed Trinity.

Once completed, step back and visualize a bright white light emanating from each tool, blessing them with Divine protection, then release your visualization, allowing it to flow into the Universe.

The Book of Shadows & Light

"There is always light in the darkness.
I will love the light, for it shows
me the way. Yet, I will endure the darkness
For it shows me the stars." Og Mandino

A Book of Shadows is a private spiritual journal that each Wiccan keeps. It was once known as a grimoire in ceremonial magick and pre-Gardnerian forms of the Craft. In British Traditional Witchcraft, each coven has an elaborate hand-written book with its origins, founders, beliefs, and bylaws. This book holds the beliefs, rituals, and ethics belonging to the tradition. As part of a mentor's responsibility to the initiate, they transcribe their student's Book of Shadows on either the day of initiation or at the end of one year and a day of solar study. The owner protects and cherishes this magickal journal and all it contains.

Before the Craft's emancipation, rumors swirled that practitioners would be buried with their magickal journals if they weren't passed down to relatives in the Craft. These books were hurriedly eradicated by family members who opposed their practices. Fear of Church authorities or local parishioners uncovering the journal's mystifying secrets was rampant throughout Europe and early New England, thinking sorcery was an unacceptable hereditary predisposition.

For Trinitarian Wicca, I chose the name Book of Shadows and Light. This phrase references Hermetic principles, the driving forces behind all of nature, the physical and metaphysical alike. It speaks of the hidden Mysteries that shadows represent as well as spiritual light, which will illuminate the path towards enlightenment, self-fulfillment, and ultimately achieving the Great Work.

Pursuing unity with the creative forces, attunement with nature, and cosmic balance is at the core of Trinitarian Wicca's spiritual goals; journaling them is part of the methodology. With cosmic balance comes patience, understanding of the laws of nature, growth in wisdom, and selfless love. All act as one and share their gifts as equals.

Until you create a more formal Book of Shadows, spiral or loose-leaf notebooks, adding scraps of paper with little phrases or thoughts written on them: rituals, spells, odes, and poetry. As we progress in the Craft, many of us have multiple grimoires—the possibilities and the contents are limitless and as vast as the Universe.

Your spiritual journal is a reference book for documenting your progress in the Craft, including herbal remedies, oils, stones, and homeopathic treatments. It's a place to write out rituals, power thoughts, blessings, spells, magickal workings, and inspiration. Everyone's book is unique!

Make your Book of Shadows and Light informational and visually pleasing with colored pens and illustrations that symbolize your beliefs or personal vision of the Blessed Trinity. Be sure to include information such as candle colors associated with specific days of the week and months of the year; herbs often used for certain rituals or reasons; moon phases; Sabbats; planetary associations; astrological correspondences; sacred symbols; talismanic seals; sigils; charms; chants and prayers associated with desired goals.

Additional recommendations: copy the magical alphabets for future reference, passages from the Conjugations of King Solomon and the planetary seals, quotes from the Gnostic Gospels, the Dead Sea Scrolls, and notes on the Kabbalah. Allow your creativity to take control and become a magical artist, decorating the pages of your grimoire with visuals that inspire you. As no two individuals are alike, your magickal journal should contain information about the Craft and ideas that have deeply affected your heart, mind, and spirit. Your magickal journal should showcase your spiritual interpretations, beliefs, and ethics about Trinitarian Wicca.

Where do I start?

Are you new to Trinitarian Wicca and unsure how to get started? If you have begun inquiring about Wicca, reading, and exploring related topics, your journey as a Wiccan has already commenced!

You may find yourself taking a detour from reading to watching Hollywood's interpretation in movies like *The Craft*, *Practical Magic*, and *The Covenant*. Don't be embarrassed if you have memorized the reruns of *Charmed* by heart—you are on your journey toward seeking answers to all your witchy questions! This shows your eagerness to learn; your quest is the hunger of a seeker, and you have left no stone unturned. It is safe to say you are on the path to becoming a Wiccan.

Here are some ideas to get you on your way. 1) Continue to seek forgotten wisdom, researching and jotting down your insights; 2) Begin a magickal diary; 3) Complete the basic Wicca quiz in this section. Be sure to write down the questions and your answers in your Book of Shadows and Light; 4) When the time feels right, pick out a Craft name for yourself; 5) Once you're ready, conduct a dedication ceremony; 6) Assemble your altar and collect all the tools you will need; and 7) Formally consecrate those tools.

Basic Wicca Quiz

1. How do you define Wicca?

2. Who is considered the founder of Wicca?

3. List as many traditions of Wicca as possible and briefly describe the ones familiar to you.

4. Describe the Deity structure in Wicca.

5. Why are you drawn to Trinitarian Wicca?

6. What is the Wiccan Rede, and what does it mean to you?

7. What is the purpose of an altar?

8. List as many items as possible usually found on the altar and their purpose.

9. What is a Book of Shadows and Light?

10. What is the purpose of casting a Circle for Wiccan rituals?

11. List the cardinal directions or the Quarters and any correspondences that come to mind.

12. What is the Wheel of the Year?

13. Name the sabbats and make a note of a phrase or keywords that help you to remember each.

14. What is your favorite sabbat, and why?

15. How many full moons are in a calendar year?

16. Are there any names of the full moons that you always remember?

17. How do you feel about the three-fold law and karma?

18. What is a familiar?

19. Are you currently working with tarot cards, oracles, a pendulum, runes, spirit boards, or other methods of divination?

20. What do you hope to gain spiritually in the next year and a day?

The solitary Wiccan community is growing at an ever-increasing rate. Without a tradition-oriented coven and the guidance of a mentor, there may be times of isolation, and you may not always know the answers. However, when you discover them for yourself, the knowledge is yours alone. At first, this may feel awkward; regardless, it will emphasize the seeker's voyage of self-discovery.

The Garden of Eden
The Summerland of Trinitarian Wicca

We are stardust, we are golden, we are billion-year-old
carbon, and we got to get ourselves back to the
Garden. — Woodstock, Crosby, Stills, Nash & Young

The British Traditional Wicca painted a picture of Summerland as a lush and beautiful place filled with magnificent gardens, meadows, and rivers. This imagery served to exemplify the indisputable connection between spirituality and nature. Nevertheless, this concept was overshadowed by eclectic Wicca and the Judeo-Christian culture in the United States, making it more of a background topic.

In contrast, Trinitarian Wicca acknowledges the beauty of recognizing a realm of perfect unity where humans and nature live in harmony. Drawing on depictions of Eden as an everlasting paradise of blissful joy, Trinitarian Wicca sees it as an eternal haven for those who have passed.

When we think of Eden, we first think of the dwelling place of Adam and Eve before their expulsion from Paradise. But there is so much more to take into consideration. It represents a perfect world with a perpetual state of innocence and flawlessness, free from sorrow and suffering, pain or death. In this context, Eden symbolizes the final resting place for humans longing for a tranquil reprieve. It brings solace and optimism to those who believe in the idea, providing comfort in the face of mortality. Whether viewed as a literal place or a metaphorical representation of spiritual fulfillment, Eden conveys unending peace and bliss.

Trinitarian Wicca aligns Eden with the Great Mother, as personified in Doreen Virtue's *Charge of the Goddess*. By recognizing that our origin and end are connected with the Goddess, we manifest this divine correlation through Eden.

To thou who thinkest to seek Me, know that
Thy seeking and yearning
Shall avail thee not unless thou knowest the Mystery.
If that which thou seekest thou findest not within thee,

Thou wilt never find it without.
For behold,
I have been with you from the beginning, and
I am that which is attained at the end of desire.

The Garden of Eden is not simply an imaginary, picturesque landscape; it embodies the unity of the soul and represents spiritual oneness. Many religious and spiritual traditions believe in a utopian life in the form of paradise at the end of our time on Earth, a place of refuge offering eternal rest. Trinitarian Wiccans refer to this realm as Eden, envisioning it as the goal of spiritual development and the ultimate destination. Eden symbolizes the transition from the physical realm to the celestial, a sign of recognition and accomplishment.

The Garden of Eden represents an ascended level of awareness in a non-corporeal form. It serves as the source of humankind's collective unconscious. To Trinitarian Wiccans, the Garden of Eden represents superior awareness in an incorporeal form. This serves as the source of humankind's subconscious. It holds an enigmatic fascination for many, like dream pieces that cannot be entirely remembered. Eden symbolizes forgotten wisdom and ancient information from a higher realm, suggesting the location of the Akashic Records. It denotes a place where peace and love are the primary governing principles.

Eden is a direct connection between humanity and the Elohim, the gateway to the celestial realm described in Genesis. It is the dwelling place of the Supernal Goddess, known by distinct names in divergent customs. It is the womb of the Underworld and a portal to the Universe, encircled by the Goddess's path and the journey of Alpha and Omega. Eden embodies the birth and death of all life, providing a sanctuary for Light Bodies, marking the end of the cycle of reincarnation.

The Garden of Eden is shrouded in mystery and has captured the imagination of people for centuries. The world's fascination with the Middle East particularly extends beyond its oil reserves, as many seek to uncover the location of this mythical paradise. Even today, numerous attempts exist to locate the Garden of Eden, from expeditions using modern technology to searches in ancient writings and folktales. Similar to quests for the Holy Grail or the Ark of the Covenant, the pursuit of sacred artifacts is driven by the desire for personal empowerment.

We must remember that everything we learn, think, or teach is based on educated guesses. No one has passed from the physical realm and returned to tell us what happens after death. Whether it is a physical location, a state of consciousness, or a frequency, it is up to each of us to decide. Do whatever brings joy and pleasure as long as it doesn't cause harm. The afterlife will come soon enough!

Rituals Explained

This section explains the diagram for solar and lunar rites and the purpose behind each part. The following rituals are not dogmatic; they are merely suggestions. Wiccan observances have specific energies and themes but are adaptable to your spiritual needs.

These rituals can be performed by an individual or a group. A solitary may wish to reduce the length of the rite, whereas Circles may assign certain tasks to specific members. If the Circle doesn't have a designated priestess or priest, then one person, a facilitator, is responsible for directing the flow of the ritual and shepherding the progression of the observance.

Self-Purification

Ritual bathing has been essential to many spiritual traditions worldwide. The purpose is to cleanse physically and spiritually, washing away mundane energies and negativity that can be collected from work, school, or daily tasks. Daily bathing is a luxury to which our generation is accustomed, as well as the convenience of indoor plumbing. In the past, only special occasions warranted a bath. These cleansing rituals are undoubtedly associated with the axiom, "Cleanliness is next to Godliness."

The most effective purification bath is one without interruptions. Silence your cell phone and tell others you will be busy for the evening. A simple purification bath by candlelight with incense sets a mystical mood for your upcoming ritual. I suggest using 7-day jar candles, which are safe and can easily be placed to enhance the atmosphere.

To begin a ritual bath, remove jewelry and clothing, casting a Circle around the area before cleansing. Add herbs such as rose petals, lavender, thyme, mint, or chamomile to the water to enhance the desired mindset; include a handful of salt to represent the Earth element.

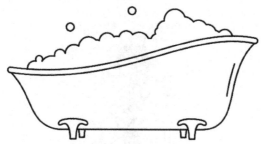

Affirmations can be spoken to help focus on your intentions for your goal. Then relax and submerge into the sanctified waters while visualizing all negative energies washing away from your body and aura.

Afterward, close off the circle when finished and respond with gratitude towards whatever awaits you next. Ritual baths can be used with other rituals or by themselves to feel spiritually cleansed after a hard day's work or before an important event. There are no rules regarding what herbs must be used and how much time should be submerged in water. What matters most is that your experience is personal, meaningful, and thoughtful for it to be truly effective.

Prepare the Invisible Body

Preparing your mind begins with physical purification. It does help a person transition from a mundane state of mind to a mystical frame of mind to accomplish the ritual's goals. Relaxing, centering, and grounding slow down our emotions and increase our ability to focus and concentrate.

Centering is a focal technique to gather emotions and control the swirling energies by balancing the concentric point where your body's weight is distributed equally. Most people suggest the plexus area, but your center can reach upward to your heart or down to your sacral chakra.

It's easiest to think of it between your breastbone and belly button. One way to determine its place is to think of something beautiful, a place you enjoy going to, your pet, or anything that gives you self-satisfaction. The location of that fluctuating warm spot is your *center*. Centering is the ability to bring all four metaphysical bodies together: the physical, mental, emotional, and spiritual.

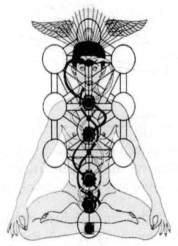

Take a deep breath in through the nose and out through the mouth. Even slow and rhythmic for the first three, and on the fourth breath, inhale deeply and hold it as long as you can before exhaling slowly and evenly.

Chanting is another powerful tool to create a mental atmosphere for rituals, spellwork, and meditation. It is a way of focusing one's internal energy and aligning oneself with the spiritual world. Repeating a phrase or stanza with a consistent rhythm allows you to control and align your body's natural energy and enter a mystical state appropriate for any ritual.

To begin chanting, start by finding a comfortable position, whether sitting or standing, with your spine straight but relaxed. Take deep breaths until you feel yourself sink into the moment. Then, begin chanting at a comfortable pace. Start slow in a whisper, allowing yourself to increase the volume of your voice as your pitch searches for a tone that resonates throughout your body.

Some people find specific mantras or phrases more effective than others, depending on their personal energies, so it is important to experiment until you find what works best. This is one I wrote for myself:

Tree of Life Chant

I am the Tree of Life
I anchor my problems and
My strife:
My roots go down,
Down into the ground,
My roots go down,
Down, down, down.

I am mercy, and I am light
I prepare for this mystic rite
My roots go down,
Down into the ground,
My roots go down,
Down, down, down.

I am severity, and I am dark
I shed negativity, just like my bark.
My roots go down,
Down into the ground,
My roots go down

Down, down, down.

I am balanced, and I am Mild
I know peace like a child.
My roots go down,
Down into the ground,
My roots go down,
Down, down, down.

Purification of the Area

Outdoor Circles require little attention as nature cleanses and purifies itself. However, removing trash or unsightly items will assist in the ritual focus. Some symbolically cleanse the indoors with the elements, like preparing for an outdoor Circle, lightly sprinkling the area with consecrated water, and wafting a stick of incense or a sage wand.

Wiccans often use a besom, a handmade broom, to sweep negativity away from the designated sacred area. The broom never touches the ground; it is a symbolic spiritual sweep.

Spiritually cleansing a space is an integral part of any ritual. In outdoor circles, nature does most of the cleansing and purifying for you. However, removing anything seen as unsightly will help limit distractions during the ritual.

To spiritually cleanse an indoor area, lightly sprinkle it with blessed water, wafting incense, or a sage wand to disperse negative energy while evoking positive influences. Wiccans often use a besom, a homemade broom, to remove negative energy from the sacred space. The ritual is called 'spiritual sweeping' because the broom never touches the ground. To perform this ritual:

Begin by focusing on your intention to remove negativity and clutter from your sacred space. Starting at the front entrance, take slow, clockwise rotations around your circle, sweeping inward towards its center, visualizing all negativity being removed as you go.

As you sweep each corner, acknowledge it out loud with words like "Negativity Go" and "Positivity Flow," or "Negativity Leave" and Positivity Receive." Once you have completed one rotation around the Circle, visualize all remaining negative energy being swept outwards from its center. Then, take one last sweep clockwise around your Circle, giving thanks for a cleansed space before placing your besom in its usual place.

To make your own holy water, simply place a pinch or two of salt into a bowl of water, activating the elements of water and earth, then raise it toward the heavens and speak your blessing request:

> *"I call upon the Blessed Trinity to bless and*
> *Consecrate this water and this salt for the*
> *Elemental purification of this Circle.*
> *Representing the Great Mother:*
> *Salt of the Earth and water of the Sea*
> *So As I will it, So Mote It Be!"*

To sanctify the incense, activating the elements of air and fire, light the incense stick, sage, or herbs on coals toward the heavens and speak your blessing request:

> *"I call upon the Blessed Trinity to bless and*
> *Consecrate this fire and this incense for the*
> *Elemental Purification of our Circle.*
> *Representing the Great Father:*
> *Flame and Fire, Air and Smoke*
> *Elemental energies, I invoke."*

Ritual Clothing

At first, you may be hesitant to wear a ceremonial outfit, especially considering it is time-consuming. However, this is not about fashion. These items help to put us in the right spiritual frame of mind. For esbats, wearing something as simple as black tights and a tunic or oversized t-shirt is more than enough; for sabbats, wearing some brightly colored garments that suit the holiday mood.

Likewise, ritual jewelry is critical to the ceremony. Many people cannot wear items that express their spirituality in public settings; thus, using oversized necklaces, rings, bracelets, or wrist cuffs specifically during rituals amplifies their value and sacredness.

Ritual jewelry is equally important. Some people have a job or family that prevents them from wearing articles of their faith, so ritual time can be more valuable. Also, oversized necklaces, rings, bracelets, or wrist cuffs may be inappropriate for everyday wear, making them extra special for rituals.

During the summer, some Wiccans prefer to wear lightweight robes and avoid heavier fabrics like velvet. For solitaries, it is up to them if they feel called to perform rituals skyclad or without clothing. In some magickal groups, they choose minimal underclothes and a season-appropriate robe.

Take into consideration that molten wax, fire, and ash can easily affect ritual clothing. You can wear your most comfortable shoes or go barefoot while dancing. Bohemian skirts and gypsy shirts may look fantastic when looking in the mirror. However, they are vulnerable to ending up in chalices of wine, bowls of water, incense ash, and candle flames at the altar or in your Circle.

Keep in mind accidents happen, even magical ones. Nevertheless, wearing special ritual attire for a solar and lunar experience inevitably adds to a beautiful spiritual connection.

Casting the Circle

Casting a Circle is the act of creating a sacred space for ritual purposes. Generally, the Circle should measure nine feet in diameter due to its numerological significance to the Goddess. This creates a separation between the mundane and spiritual planes of existence. However, it's not a protective barrier preventing lower-frequency energy from entering.

Rather than being a physical construct, the Circle is a platform to perform your rituals. Repeatedly summoning energy in one specific spot will create a power site like Stonehenge or Avebury, found in the British Isles.

Many of these sacred sites contain inexplicable sources of geomagnetic energy. We know little about the people who constructed them and their original intent. Nevertheless, these henges or circles have been used as observatories to mark seasonal change, have therapeutic benefits, and are utilized as devices for tracking constellations in the astrological year.

Often, covens who have established a long-term sacred space mark the perimeter of the Circle with stones and leave them in place. This practice is intended to capture and retain the energy generated during rituals. When entering this area, the collected energy may cause some individuals to feel tingling sensations like the atmosphere before a thunderstorm.

The Circle is an area of sacredness; however, the description is a bit inaccurate. This area does not have two sides but rather three—it is spherical. Close your eyes and imagine the top half of the circle as a dome extending over the space with its reflection curving beneath the earth. Those standing directly in this space would view a rainbow between 90 and 180 degrees, yet those in an airplane could witness the entire 360-degree arc of the rainbow.

Some individuals can see the bluish-white energy of the Circle, while others can visualize it. You can create or cast this Circle using an athame, a wand, or your index finger—whatever method works best for you.

Trinitarian Wiccans can best interpret the energy current in a sacred space using the alchemical symbol for the Philosopher's Stone or the circle squared. The circumference of a circle represents the Sacred Space. The triangle is the threefold energy flow of the Blessed Trinity. The square represents the material world and the four elements: earth, air, fire, and water. The Inner Circle represents the energy of the practitioner.

The outer circle represents the macrocosm (the universe or cosmos), and the innermost circle represents the Microcosm (humanity).

*"As above, so below, as within, so without, as the universe, so the soul...." **Hermes Trismegistus***

The human soul is as vast as the universe, and their parallels are inextricable. In the diagram below, Robert Fludd illustrates humanity's place in the universe. According to Fludd,

*"**Man is a whole world of its own, called a microcosm, for it displays a miniature pattern of all the parts of the universe. Thus, the head is related to the Empyreal, the chest to the ethereal heaven, and the belly to the elementary substance.**"*

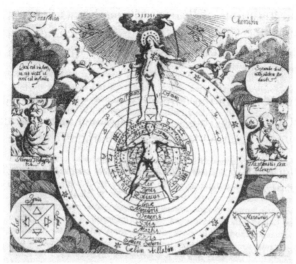

The sacred space is a non-physical temple and a natural sanctuary. As the Gnostic Gospel of Thomas explains, the Divine *"is not in a building made of wood or stone; split a piece of wood, and I am there; lift a stone, and you will find me."* Trinitarian Wicca reveres the Circle as a sacred space and gives it the same respect a member of another belief system would display to their church, temple, or tabernacle.

During rituals, feeling comfortable with your environment helps bring out the energy in your circle. With practice, you will become more at ease and more likely to discover the power within. Tingles may begin at your fingertips, while your palms could heat up as you manipulate energy. It isn't unheard of for your own voice to give you goosebumps as you speak devotional parts aloud. You might even get misty-eyed or shed a tear over how strong your emotions are when lighting a candle or smelling familiar incense. If this happens, it's evidence of getting into the spirit of the rite.

The Challenge

The Challenge is part of a group ritual symbolic of inquiry of trust and intent among the participants in the Circle. The beauty of ritual symbolism is crucial to all traditions of Wicca. Although outsiders may misconstrue it as threatening, the Challenge signifies one's choice to join the Circle willingly, intending to connect with other individuals of like mind in perfect love and trust.

Those already within the Circle choose someone to hold the athame towards the guests respectfully. The challenger speaks a single question to those wishing to enter. One of the most famous examples is:

> **"It is better to rush upon this blade than to enter the Circle with fear or hatred in your heart. How do you enter?"**

An appropriate reply is:

> **"In Perfect Love and Perfect Trust."**

The participants form a line at the East Gate, waiting for the challenge to enter the Circle. Once inside, they find their assigned places around the altar or along the parameter.

As more Wiccan groups have formed and eclectics gather to host Circles, it's become common to use a short challenge-and-response ritual. However, many Circles have abandoned this practice altogether.

Entering the Circle

Anointing participants with oils is a common practice in many world religions. It often represents a miniature rededication to the Divine and personal purification before entering the Sacred Space. Again, it is a symbol of reclaimed baptism before each ritual.

Trinitarian Wicca has a Jewish mysticism background, so the Kabbalistic Cross sign works well for an anointing or self-anointing gesture. The cross has been the symbol of protecting the heart chakra or chest cavity, once believed to be the soul's dwelling place.

The Kabbalistic Cross uses the Solar Cross, which has equal arms vertically and horizontally, indicating the balance of the universe's male and female forces. The four points dictate the placement of the words

"Ateh, Malkuth, ve-Geburah, ve-Gedulah, le Olam. Amen." This is Hebrew for "Thine is the Kingdom, the Power, and the Glory Forever, Amen."

It's a customary blessing. Place your hand on your forehead and intone, "Ah-tay," which means "For Thine...[is]; touch the top of your abdomen/heart area and say, "Mol-Koot, " which means "the Kingdom," touch your right shoulder and say, "Vih-G'boo-Rah," meaning "[and] the Power," and touch your left shoulder and say "Vih-G'dew-Lah" which means "[and] the Glory." Now clasp your hands together in a prayer gesture and say, "Lah-Oh-Lahm Ah-Mane," which means "Forever, Amen."

Calling the Quarters

Calling the Quarters invokes the elements associated with the cardinal directions. Beings known as the Watchers are assigned to guard each Quarter, serving as protectors of the Watchtowers and the elemental forces they embody.

Air and Fire are typically seen as masculine elements. In the east, pale to mid-yellow represents air; these hues are associated with intelligence, invention, and productivity. Meanwhile, the south is usually expressed in vibrant reds due to its association with the element of fire and emotions such as passion and rage.

Trinitarian Wiccans recognize celestial and terrestrial forces as having gender traits, including water and earth, which are considered female elements. Cool to mid-blue is often used for the west, corresponding to its relationship to the element of water, intuition, clairvoyance, and psychic abilities. North is represented by fertile green for its ties to the element of earth and motherly nurturing characteristics, such as grounding and overall stability.

How we perceive the Guardians is determined by our beliefs. Trinitarian Wiccans may see them as angels or archangels, while others view them as dragons or fairies. No matter how we imagine the Watchers, they are sentient beings connected to elements that must be acknowledged with respect. They are present in the Circle to protect us and even have a sense of humor about our mistakes.

If you have a positive relationship with the angels, these archangels are best contacted when Calling the Quarters. Raphael is the Guardian of the East and is connected to air. Michael guards the South and symbolizes fire, Gabriel oversees the West and water, and Uriel watches over the North, representing Earth.

Calling the Quarters serves two functions. Firstly, it guards the consecrated space and those within it against unwanted energies that may attach themselves to the power being conjured. Secondly, each Quarter's unique energy lends strength to magnify each practitioner's mystical desires.

When conjuring the Watchtowers, each person will imagine them differently. In my mind's eye, they look like 17-foot-tall turrets of a castle surrounded by a mist with hues of North (green), East (pale yellow or off-white), South (vibrant red), and West (light blue).

When invoking the Watchtowers, it is important to know their correspondences and incorporate them into the Quarter Call. For example, affiliations when invoking the Archangel Raphael to the Watchtowers of the East might include:

"Hail to the Archangel Raphael,
Keeper of the Watchtowers of the East,
Element of Air influencing
Creativity and intelligence
Guardian of good health and
Celestial healing:
I invoke thee!
Welcome!"

Invocation of the Blessed Trinity

The Invocation is performed to gain an audience with the Divine. Wiccans believe in one God/dess who exists everywhere and in everyone. Trinitarian Wiccans invoke the Mother-Father Deity Elohim, the Blessed Trinity, or other members of the Elohian pantheon. There is no separation between oneself and Deity; you are part of the unified whole. Invocation is not an attempt to control Deities but a hospitable invitation to come into your life.

The meaning of invocation, especially regarding Deity, is drawing/inviting the Divine into you. This means drawing energy into yourself from where it already exists—inside of you. The first-century Christians devoutly believed that the Divine "is inside you and all around you," as stated in the Gospel of Thomas. Trinitarian Wiccans hold a similar belief because we are each little gods and goddesses.

If the Divine already resides within us, why invite them in? This can be best explained using a magnetic field analogy: this invisible force is capable of immense power. Invocation acts as an inductive power to link humanity and the Divine. The stronger your magnetic field, the farther it reaches out. So, the more heartfelt and earnest your prayers for communion with the Divine, the greater the chance of spiritual connection, answered petitions, attainment of goals, and inner tranquility.

Statement of Purpose

In a group setting, The Statement of Purpose is when the Circle's orator introduces themselves, welcomes the guests, acknowledges the regular participants, and announces the purpose of the gathering, whether it is an Esbat, Kyriat, or a Sabbat. This introduction is meant to be motivational and set a positive tone for the ritual. This step is unnecessary in solitary practice, as the individual knows the reason for the rite.

During my Dianic Wicca studies, I was taught that the Circle's energy builds from the moment of announcement. Stating the intention brings mental focus and concentration to start building power. The power continues to grow throughout the ritual until it reaches its most potent point at chanting or other means of coning the energy.

The Body of the Ritual

The body of the ritual is the heart of the ceremony, making it either a joyous observance or a powerful magickal work. However, this is the hardest part of Wicca to explain thoroughly. Many books provide explanations of the sabbats, instructions on casting a Circle, calling the Quarters, and invoking the Lord & Lady or Blessed Trinity. Then, they reverse these processes.

Although seekers may not have a mentor to assist them, you can soon create meaningful solar and lunar rites with regular practice without one. The components of esbats and sabbats differ; nevertheless, some devotees incorporate solar and lunar elements into their rituals.

Group rituals may involve theatrical re-enactments, such as passing through a veil and descending into the Underworld on Samhain. Foot-washing at Midsummer can be done by a solitary practitioner or with a group. Depending on your circumstances, a feast or potluck might be appropriate to celebrate Mabon; if you choose to keep it private, conduct the ceremony before having guests over. For Beltane and Lammas, crafting items like corn dollies, yule logs, besoms, sun wheels, and crowns for the May Queen or Corn King, respectively, is an option. Rituals don't only involve physical actions: if you find yourself drawn to writing prose and poetry, let Edgar Allan Poe inspire your Samhain celebrations.

Magickal workings are the mystical activities of the esbats. Because lunar energy is abundant on full moons, it unlocks our subconscious mind and activates our psychic faculties. During the lunar phases, esoteric efforts tend to come naturally. They boost personal energy and focus on our will. As a result, esbats are the best time for spell work for healing, love, or money. This body of the ritual is mystical and internal, allowing divination to flow uninhibited. Magickal workings also include empowering charms, talismans, and charging crystals.

Once the dedicant becomes familiar with the multiple story arcs that play out during the Wheel of the Year, begin changing up the details of the sabbats by adding your own creative ideas. This allows for personalizing your mystical growth and helps prevent ritual fatigue.

Raising and Releasing Power

Trinitarian Wiccans use energy in the Circle to make their magical acts and rituals more powerful. This can be done in different ways, such as vibrating a single word or God-name, humming, chanting, and drumming. The combination of sound and repetition brings the focus from conscious to unconscious, which helps produce alpha waves that put one in a trance-like state. Everyone is born with inner power, which Wiccans learn to sense, control, increase, enhance, and release during rituals.

To raise energy, start by bringing your hands up from your sides until they are over your head. You may feel resistance when you reach about halfway up – that's the weight of the collected energy. As you continue raising your arms, it will become heavier and heavier, like slowly lifting an invisible beach ball that weighs ten or fifteen pounds!

It is incredible to experience, but it is expected to feel temporary aches in the shoulders and elbows. When this is done in a group, this weight is amplified. Feeling a strain on your shoulders and arms is natural when performing a group ritual. Usually, this feeling will pass once the energy is released towards the intention of the ceremony. Describing all the emotions and sensations of raising power is difficult; it's different for everyone. A novice might anticipate something more theatrical than what they will actually experience. Regardless, what we are really doing is harnessing the energies of nature around us: the Earth itself, the four elements, and both lunar and solar influences. It's possible to sense these forces even with our eyes closed and minds at ease.

Rituals of chanting and dancing are not limited to Wicca; they can be found throughout various cultures, such as Native American, Afro-Caribbean, Australian Aboriginal, and shamanistic. You should choose the rhythm and cadence that works best for you: drums, singing, chanting, clapping of hands, or the stamping of feet. It does not matter if your chants are perfect or not. Visualize the words as images in your head while you chant. Allow these images to create an energy flow. For example,

*"I feel the energy flowing to me, flowing like a river to
the sea. I feel the energy flowing up from the ground,
flowing down from the sky, flowing around and around."*

As the intensity grows, it is natural to speed up your motion. You may
find yourself chanting, dancing, twirling, drumming, or clapping faster
and faster. Eventually, you'll know you have reached the peak of energy
raising. Your actions will often take over in a wild show of celebration. If
you are with others, pick a word or phrase, such as *"down!"* and suddenly
drop to your knees. Just before things get out of control—shout the release
word and envision the desired outcome. Warning: Giggling and
uncontrollable laughter may happen!

The Great Rite

The Great Rite celebrates the Divine Union of the God and Goddess,
symbolically using the Chalice and Athame. The Chalice symbolizes the
womb of the Goddess, while the athame represents the phallus of the God.
Uniting these tools acknowledges the balance of male and female
energies. Trinitarian Wiccans place the athame attentively in the chalice
as it is seen as the original act of creation from where life originates. As
the athame and chalice are joined together, visualize the union of the God
and Goddess within, which activates the Divine Spark, encouraging an
uplifted sense of self-worth, acceptance, and unity with nature, leading to
spiritual transformation. Trinitarian Wiccans acknowledge this symbolic
act as the Sacred Marriage or Hieros Gamos.

The Great Rite stems from the importance of fertility rituals practiced
by various cultures. These rituals were performed to ensure the fertility of
the land, crops, and animals and to achieve the positive goals of
procreation. The Great Rite is a physical act and part of the individual's
spiritual journey. It represents the union of opposites, the merging of the
conscious and subconscious, and the integration of the divine within
oneself. Through this ritual, Wiccans seek to achieve personal
transformation and spiritual growth. Participating in the Great Rite allows
practitioners to tap into their inner power, embrace their Higher Selves,
and establish and strengthen their Divine connection.

The Great Rite can be performed using three taper candles or a wedding candle set. Light the two external flames for the God and Goddess, then use both the bride's and groom's candles to light the middle one, symbolizing their unity in marriage.

Feast and Libations

Cakes and Ale is a part of the ritual that symbolizes unity between the spiritual and physical world. The food stands for the physical nourishment we receive while also providing an offering to the Blessed Trinity. This act simultaneously feeds us both physically and spiritually.

Cakes represent the element of Earth and the physical nourishment they provide. Ale represents the element of Water, which sustains our emotional body. Together, these items represent equilibrium between our four bodies: mental, physical, emotional, and spiritual; a connection with Deity is cultivated. Ingesting Cakes and Ale is communion with the Divine Feminine and Masculine, establishing an intimate relationship, attesting to their existence in the ceremony, and asking for their favor. These offerings are blessed with Divinity's energy and nature, enabling Trinitarian Wiccans to absorb their insight, power, and rewards.

Baking bread has been a sign of fellowship, friendliness, and solidarity throughout history. We share food with others to show our commitment to them or to mend broken relations between former enemies. Eating together is an ancient ritual that symbolizes inner faithfulness, promises, unity, and growth.

Consuming Cakes and Ale after a ritual helps restore balance in the body by lowering energy levels raised inside the Circle. As a product of nature, the food brings awareness back to its usual level, a process often described as *"earthing the power."*

During an Esbat ritual, Cakes and Ale signify the blessings and support given by the Great Mother. Individuals can take in the lunar energies and become one with the Divine Feminine by partaking in these offerings. At a Sabbat, however, the consecration of Cakes and Ale is imbued with the characteristics of that particular festival governed by the Solar Lord.

At Samhain, edible and drinkable offerings are made to honor ancestors and spirits. For Trinitarian Wiccans, these rituals connect the living and the dead. The offerings solidify the bond between both realms and create a sense of continuity.

In an Esbat ritual, Cakes and Ale symbolize the blessings and guidance imparted by the Great Mother. Consuming these offerings allows individuals to absorb the lunar energies and connect with the Divine Feminine. During a Sabbat, the consecration of Cakes and Ale takes on the qualities of the festival guided by the Solar Lord.

Journal Your Thoughts

It is vital to document the outcomes of your esoteric journey. Whether you have just completed a ceremony, meditated deeply, used divination, taken a leisurely walk through nature, or jotted down a dream, capture your insights in great detail when they are still clear and unsullied. It is best to journal the experience before it becomes distorted by imagination and misremembered as fact.

Keeping track of the time, date, location, and any external conditions that may affect your work is essential. Make a note of anything unexpected that could influence its outcome, whether positive or negative. Ensure you write down your experiences as clearly as possible so you can refer to them later. It is unnecessary to be overly exacting in your journal; record your feelings and general impressions, too.

The purpose of journaling is to chart your progress, results, and techniques for achieving this spiritual growth. This will allow you to review how far you've come and assess your development. We all progress on our journeys but often don't realize it until we look back at our experiences. This includes rituals, divination, spellcraft, and dreams.

Thanking the Blessed Trinity

When calling on the energies of the Blessed Trinity to join you in your sacred space, it is essential to be mindful and reverent. The invocation should be made with care and sincerity. It can be more elaborate or as simple as:

> **"I invite the Blessed Trinity to enter my Circle and share in my ritual today."**

This invocation should draw on your spiritual connection, not just your intellectual understanding of their roles. Once your ritual is complete, thank them for joining you; this might sound something like:

> **"Thank you for being here with me today. I am grateful for your presence, power, and what you have brought to this ritual."**

Invite the Blessed Trinity to stay if they desire or go if they must. It is appropriate to invite the Blessed Trinity to *"stay if you will, go if you must."* This allows them to remain within your sacred space or depart when their work is done. Acknowledge their energies have been powerful guides throughout the ritual by expressing gratitude once more before concluding it entirely.

During these rituals, the energy exchange between yourself and the Blessed Trinity creates a connection that can last long after its conclusion. It also provides a chance for personal growth through reflection. Self-reflection on experiences shared during ritual work helps us appreciate what we have learned from each moment spent with them. Remember that even though we may not always understand how our paths align with theirs in those moments, we must recognize their presence in our lives as teachers and protectors.

Dismissing the Quarters

It is called Dismissing the Quarters, but it is the ritualistic release of the four elements: earth, air, fire, and water. These elements are seen as possessing qualities of sentience, infusing powerful resources into your rituals. It should be noted that these elements belong to no one spiritual tradition or faith; thus, they shouldn't be kept longer than necessary in such ceremonies. After all, they have other places to go and things to do!

The Quarters are dispersed opposite of how they were summoned at the East Gate. The release will start at the North Gate, thanking the element of Earth for being present, whatever their form was. Acknowledge any characteristics or references used when you initially greeted them. It is acceptable to just thank them and offer hospitality by saying, *"Stay if you will, go if you must."*

Dismissing the Circle

There is no need to hasten the end of the ritual just because it is finished. The area has been purified and infused with personal and Divine energy, so this is a Good time to stay inside the Circle to relish in its accumulated power and meditate. Suggested Circle Closing statements:

I call this Circle open but never broken,
Make the love of the Blessed Trinity be forever in my heart!
Merry Meet and Merry Part, And Merry Meet Again!
Blessed Be!

Finally, take care of all items used in your ritual; anything borrowed should be returned, and personal tools or altarpieces should be wiped and put away appropriately. Once you have finished putting the area back in order, step away from your sacred space, knowing it has been restored to its natural state.

First Ritual Jitters

Our doubts are treacherous, and for them,
we lose the good that we could often win
for fear of trying. ----- William Shakespeare

It's natural to be a bit anxious before your first ritual—whether within the confines of your home or a public event. The first few rituals can be daunting, but that's true for everyone; it's not an indication from the gods or any other divine being, just human fear.

Everyone wants their first ritual to go flawlessly. However, you can unintentionally put too much pressure on yourself by tending to the little details that will eventually become second nature. Many of us have made clumsy mistakes, such as spilling the chalice of wine, dropping and breaking our favorite one-of-a-kind clay bowls, or even throwing our athame while casting a Circle.

Then comes the difficulties with ritual clothing. Yes, they are essential to take on your role as your magickal self, but it's crucial to remember all garments can be stained or permanently smudged. Even if everything goes as planned, you may burn the hem of your summer broomstick skirt or singe the sleeve of your robe or peasant blouse.

The forces of Nature are fickle and whimsical, but it is part of that same wildness that makes our festivals and rites so invigorating and memorable. Over time, your magical journal will become smeared with candle wax, dusted with incense, and marked by fragrant oils and herbs. This is your magickal fingerprint, a testament to the work you have done for your craft, and a sign of your due diligence.

You can reduce stress by getting into a daily magickal routine and ritualizing your tasks. This practice is not limited to relieving anxiety or gaining confidence; it's living your path—this is living Wicca.

For example, you could consecrate your orange juice and toast in the morning before breakfast. Place four elemental candles around your tub for an evening bath and call upon the Quarters so that your bath is cleansing and calming. When dedicating time for meditation or devotion, light a candle for the Blessed Trinity and talk to God, Goddess, and the Solar Lord more casually for a more intimate feel.

Everyone is nervous before a significant event; transitioning from church to circle is no exception. Apprehension is expected before your first date, speaking in front of the class at school, taking your driver's test, or a job interview.

Take a few deep breaths to soothe your nerves. I promise it will be an experience you will cherish for the rest of your journey in the Craft. Trinitarian Wicca is yours to explore, develop, recover, and delight in. You'll do great — Blessed Be!

Esbats
Celebrating the Goddess

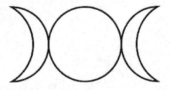

The full moon has long been associated with mystical and magical powers, revered for its heightened energy and spiritual significance. Esbats are lunar rites focusing on the Great Mother. The term esbat is of French origin, from *s'esbattre*, which loosely translates to "frolic joyfully," suggesting a night of wild energy enjoyed with one or more of the Elohian Goddesses.

The full moon is plentiful with power, and rituals can be created and adapted to fit one's individual goals. Celebrations of this special night include honoring the Goddess, visualizing goals for oneself or others, making offerings of food or wine, giving thanks for all of life's gifts, casting spells for manifesting desires, and reflecting on personal growth since the last full moon. Esbats can help us connect with our inner selves, provide spiritual guidance, and give us insight into our destinies or directions in life.

This 28-day lunar cycle is essential to female participants; it can balance spiritual and physical bodies. When a woman's physical body mirrors her moon phase by experiencing menstruation at the time of the full moon, synchronization can reduce discomfort, improve fertility, and uplift overall feminine health and well-being.

The phases of the visible Moon reflect the Goddess: the Maiden, Mother, and Crone. The archetypes symbolize the different cyclic stages of a woman's life. By connecting with these phases, practitioners gain a deeper understanding of the Divine Feminine as it applies to their own personal journey.

At the New Moon, we plant the seeds of our hopes and desires. It's an excellent opportunity to draw up wishes for the month ahead and set an overall intention for what we want to manifest in our lives. During this phase, we should focus on cleansing, clearing away any obstacles that may stand in our way of receiving abundance.

The Waxing Moon is a time for positive growth as everything comes alive with energy. We can nourish our goals, dreams, and intentions with affirmations and visualization.

The Full Moon is a powerful time when energy peaks in intensity. We can use this power to manifest our deepest desires if they serve us positively and honor our ethical guidelines.

The Waning Moon helps us release any unwanted or negative emotions holding us back from achieving our highest potential. This is also a great chance to forgive others for past wrongs so we can move forward without lingering pain or resentment.

Esbats are dissimilar to sabbats, as the latter are solar festivities related to the Trinity's interaction with the ever-changing seasons: the Wheel of the Year. Esbats are for magical work and Drawing Down the Moon, a ritual where Wiccans appeal to the lunar essence of the Goddess within themselves to gain clarity, thoughtfulness, or prophecy.

The Charge of the Goddess, composed by Doreen Valiente, is an inspirational ode written in the voice of the Goddess. It is read aloud in the Circle, guaranteeing Her Children that She has always been present among us to love, teach, guide, and protect us, even while in exile.

These rituals have been written for the solitary practitioner. The first paragraphs of *Drawing Down the Moon* include a narrative intended to help guide the Goddess' essence into your body and mention some sensations you can expect to experience. The early sections of Drawing Down the Moon contain a narrative to help bring the Goddess's essence into your being and describe some feelings you may experience.

Participants raise their arms heavenward when it feels right, facing the moon. With eyes closed, call upon the Goddess in a way most comfortable for you or the group. You may feel gentle gusts of wind, a sudden sensation of heat surrounding you, or sparkles of light flittering across your vision. Without a doubt, a surreal feeling of peace and acceptance will wash over you. A tingling in your fingers, warmth in your palms, and the instinctive urge to sway are all desired responses that signal lunar energy is being absorbed smoothly.

The last section is the Five-fold Kiss, the ritualistic act of five symbolic kisses on various body parts accompanied by a blessing. Each kiss represents a specific aspect of the Divine connection between the practitioner and the sacred energies. It has been adapted as a self-anointing ritual using water or your choice of oil as you speak the five body blessings and their specific role acknowledged in Wicca.

The Kiss of the Earth is placed on the feet, symbolizing the grounding and connection to the Earth. Trinitarian Wiccans draw strength and stability by honoring the Earth. We acknowledge our dependence and interconnectivity with the planet, expressing our gratitude.

The Kiss of the Water is placed on the knees, representing the fluidity and adaptability of water. Trinitarian Wiccans embrace our constant nature of changing emotions and fluid patterns of intuition. Through this kiss, we honor the power of our feelings and their ability to guide and transform our perceptions.

The Kiss of the Fire is placed on the genitals, symbolizing fire's transformative and passionate energy. Trinitarian Wiccans can embrace our natural creativity and desire, igniting the Divine Spark within. This kiss celebrates the sacredness of sexuality, channeling our passion toward spiritual evolution.

The Kiss of the Air is placed on the lips, representing the breath of life and the power of communication. Air symbolizes intellect, inspiration, and the exchange of ideas. Through this kiss, Trinitarian Wiccans honor the importance of clear communication, the power of their words, and the sharing of wisdom to inspire and uplift others.

The Kiss of the Spirit is placed on the forehead, symbolizing the connection to the divine and the awakening of spiritual consciousness.

Trinitarian Wiccans recognize the union of our individual spirit with the Divine energies that permeate all living things.

Various traditions may use variations on the fourth kiss for spirit and the fifth for air. To rearrange the kiss and blessing, place a kiss on the chest for strength and stability and on the lips for communication and proclamation.

13 Benefits of Lunar Energy

The full moon holds a special place in our consciousness, associated with the mystical. It lights our way on our spiritual journal towards reclaiming the Goddess in Trinitarian Wicca.

The 13 magickal powers attributed to the full moon encompass many spiritual and transformative aspects, from amplifying intentions to enhancing psychic abilities and promoting healing. By embracing the full moon's energy, we tap into its potential and explore the depths of our own spiritual journey.

1. Amplification of Intentions: The lunar energy peaks during the full moon, making it an ideal time to set objectives and manifest desires. The full moon amplifies our thoughts and intentions, helping us to focus our energy and bring our desires into reality.

2. Cleansing and Releasing: The full moon is often associated with cleansing and releasing negative energy. The moon's powerful energy helps us release emotional baggage, old patterns, and anything that no longer serves us. This allows for personal growth and transformation.

3. Heightened Intuition: The full moon enhances our intuitive abilities. It heightens our psychic senses, making it easier to tap into our inner wisdom and receive guidance from the spiritual realm.

4. Healing and Nurturing: The full moon is associated with healing and nurturing energies. The moon's gentle light soothes and heals emotional wounds, promoting inner peace and well-being.

5. Enhancing Psychic Abilities: The full moon enhances our psychic abilities, clairvoyance, telepathy, and mediumship. During this time, the veil between the physical and spiritual realms is thinner, allowing for more accessible communication with the unseen.

6. Enhancing Creativity: The full moon is associated with creativity and inspiration. The moon's energy stimulates our creative flow, allowing us to tap into our artistic abilities and express ourselves more freely.

7. Balancing Energies: The full moon brings balance and harmony to our lives. The moon's energy aids in establishing equilibrium between our emotions, thoughts, and actions, promoting inner peace and alignment.

8. Enhancing Manifestation: The full moon is a powerful time for manifestation. The moon's energy can help us align with our desires and attract what we want into our lives. This includes abundance, love, and opportunities.

9. Enhancing Rituals and Spells: The full moon is considered an auspicious time for performing rituals and casting spells. The moon's energy amplifies their effectiveness, making them more potent and impactful.

10. Enhancing Dreamwork: The full moon is associated with vivid dreams, enhanced recall, and the development of the ability for dream walking. The moon's energy assists us in accessing the wisdom of our subconscious mind, providing insights and guidance through our dreams.

11. Enhancing Lunar Magick: The full moon is prime time for all forms of lunar magick. The moon's energy can be harnessed for various purposes, such as protection, divination, and spiritual growth. Practitioners of magick often perform rituals and spells during the full moon to harness its potent energy.

12. Connecting with Lunar Deities: The full moon is associated with lunar deities in mythologies worldwide. The connection is more vital now, allowing for deeper communion and receiving their blessings and guidance.

13. Celebrating and Honoring Cycles: The full moon is associated with the cycles of life and our ever-changing existence. It empowers us to embrace the ebb and flow of life's rhythms. Many cultures hold ceremonies and rituals during the full moon to honor these cycles and express gratitude for the blessings in their lives.

Full Moon Names

January—Wolf Moon: **Anath,** the Goddess of Protection from the Canaanites, is celebrated this month. The Wolf Moon is named for the ritual observance of protection and guarding the home, family, and territory. Good fortunes, change of luck, and household protection are all associated rituals with the Wolf Moon.

February—Storm Moon: **Brigid**, the Goddess of Mystic Fire from the Celts, is celebrated this month. The Storm Moon is named to acknowledge the end of the stormy nights and cold weather. This ritual helps plan for the spring, family peace, and blessing your home's boundaries.

March—Chaste Moon: Zoe, the Goddess of New Beginnings from the Gnostics, is celebrated this month. The Chaste Moon is named in recognition of Spring. All things in nature are virginal, fresh, and blooming. It is a time for new beginnings, and rituals should reflect this by warding off negative energies while planning for the warm months ahead.

April—Seed Moon: **Barbelo,** the Goddess of the Universal Womb, Trinitarian Wicca's Star Goddess from the Barbeloites of Gnostism, celebrated this month. The Seed Moon is named for the time of the sowing of seeds and their cultivation. Rituals reflect the planting of seasonal flowers and crops, acknowledging the new cycle of life. This is the time to put winter plans into action.

May—Bright Moon: Shekinah, the Goddess of Divine Light, from Hebrew mysticism. This full moon is associated with Supermoons, the moons that appear typically brighter and more prominent than usual. The increased illumination reflects the guiding brilliance of the Feminine

Divine displayed in the pillar of fire guiding the Israelites out of Egypt and the sacred flames of the Menorah.

June—Dyad Moon: Mary Magdalene, the Goddess of Love and Companionship. She has been called the Goddess of the Gospels and the "apostle to the apostles" in eclectic Christian traditions. This full moon is named after the Latin word Dyad, meaning two, indicating a pair or a set of twins. Now, the days and nights are equal in length, and nature's male and female forces are in balance. Rituals should reflect a duality.

July—Meade Moon: Asherah, the Goddess of Home and Hearth, from the Canaanites. Mother Goddess celebrated this month. This full moon recognizes the Festival of Ale in Old Europe, a time for making wines and ales from Meade. Rituals should include thanks for religious freedom and making plans for new goals.

August—Corn Moon: Guadalupe, the Goddess of the Harvest, from Mexican-American sainthood. She is so much more: Empress Mother of the Americas and matron saint of Mexico. This full moon indicates the first of the three traditional harvests. This marks the time for the beginning of canning and preserving. Rituals are bread-oriented, strongly emphasizing harvesting crops, gardens, or the good fortune of the work you have accomplished in previous months.

September—Harvest Moon: Sophia, the Goddess of Divine Wisdom from the Gnostics. This full moon is associated with the second and largest harvest of the year. This esbat is a time for an elaborate fall celebration, including the autumn equinox.

October—Blood Moon: Lilith, the Goddess of Transformation. As hunting season begins, this full moon is affiliated with blood, and animals are slaughtered to prepare food for the winter. This month is the third and final harvest. October 31 ends the Wiccan calendar, and rituals this month should deal with banishing bad habits and purifying one's life and house.

November—Snow Moon: The Holy Spirit, the Goddess of Proclamation. This full moon is named for the association of the coming of winter, symbolized by snow. The start of the season of death to the wheel of the year is a good time for reflection. Rituals should focus on the positive aspects of our lives and plan to dispose of dead weight in our physical, spiritual, and emotional experiences.

December—Oak Moon: Mother Mary, the Goddess of Fortitude. This full moon is named after the mighty oak tree, which stands strong through the winter months. The oak is a sign of strength to practitioners during the dreary winter months. Rituals of success and prosperity start from an acorn.

Random 13th Moon—Blue Moon: Levannah, the Goddess of the Ancient Moon. A blue moon is not physically blue, of course. However, an additional moon occurs when two full moons appear within a calendar month, or the third of four moons appear in a season. Because this moon is a variable, it gave rise to the saying "once in a blue moon."

Blue moons are considered lucky; magickal workings are full of positive but untamed energy; this is a perfect time for prosperity and good luck. The Blue Moon calculations began with the onset of the Gregorian calendar in October 1582; the official first recognition of a blue moon was August 21, 1937.

Materials Needed for Esbats:

The Altar should be placed at the heart of the Circle, facing the East Gate. It can be decorated with any color cloth. For example, a black and white altar cloth might symbolize the night sky and the white moon, while purples and blacks can set a mystical mood. The Trinity Candles are used in a special candle lighting ceremony using red for Jesus, white for the Father, and black for the Mother.

Silver jewelry and accessories are suggested when creating a spiritual altar, as the reflective metal is connected to the moon, aiding an individual's psychism. Silver candle holders, chalices, bread platters, and bowls for storing water and salt will all contribute to an aesthetically pleasing display. Items with silver hues and clear or white glass help to create an inspirational altar.

Other symbols associated with the moon are white flowers, salt, and moonstone. Adding seasonal blooming white flowers to the altar in the Circle adds to the central beauty. Night-blooming white flowers, such as jasmine, carnations, gardenia, lilies, iris, and white roses, make a great addition. Additionally, salt can be used to outline the perimeter of the Circle. The Gnostic *Gospel of Philip* discusses salt's key role in association with the Goddess Sophia. Salt's white hue fits the overall theme surrounding the Goddess.

The Circle is cast to create a sacred space for honoring the Great Mother and establish a platform for magickal workings, inner reflection, and divination. Its diameter measures nine feet, as the number nine is associated with the moon and the Goddess. However, this size may need to be adjusted when working indoors.

Pre-Ritual Preparation

Purification of Self: A Purification Bath with Roses
Attunement Tea: Red Raspberry Leaf Tea
Anointing Oil: Moon Oil
Incense: Sandalwood
Semi-Precious Stones: Moonstone and Amethyst

Assemble the Altar

Place the Altar in the center of the Circle
Use black and white altar cloths
A Chalice for ale, wine, or grape juice
A tray for cakes or bread

Consecrate the Area

[Add a pinch of salt to the bowl of water and hold it
toward the sky, asking this or similar blessings:]

I call upon the Blessed Trinity to
Consecrate this water and this salt for the

Elemental Purification of this Circle.
Representing my Goddess:
Of the Earth and Water of the Sea,
So as I will it, So mote it be!

[Using the flame of a candle, light the incense,
and hold it toward the sky,
asking this or similar blessings:]

I call upon the Blessed Trinity to
Consecrate this flame and
This incense for the
Elemental Purification of this Circle.
Representing my God:
By Fire and Air, Glory to Thee
So as I will it, So mote it be!

Elemental Chant
[Chant as you consecrate the Circle:]

Earth, my body;
Water my blood.
Air my breath; and
Fire my spirit.

Casting the Circle

I conjure Thee O Sacred Circle of power
In this magickal place,
At this magickal hour:
Energies merge and converge
For this Full Moon Rite!

Call the Quarters

Hail to the Guardians of the
Watchtowers of the East

Keepers of the element of Air
Influencing creativity and intelligence
Be with me this Lunar Rite
I invoke thee!
Welcome!

Hail to the Guardians of the
Watchtowers of the South
Keepers of the element of Fire
Influencing passion and will
Be with me in this Lunar Rite
I invoke thee!
Welcome!

Hail to the Guardians of the
Watchtowers of the West
Keepers of the element of Water
Influencing empathy and clairvoyance
Be with me this Lunar Rite
I invoke thee!
Welcome!

Hail to the Guardians of the
Watchtowers of the North
Keepers of the element of Earth
Influencing solidarity and fortitude
Be with me this Lunar Rite
I invoke thee!
Welcome!

The Invocation of the Goddess

Hail to the Great Goddess!
Glorious Mother of the Heavens,
O Luminous Lady Divine!
I ask you to be with me

During this full moon rite,
I feel your lunar energies
Celestial Goddess of the Night Sky.

Mother of All Living Things
You are hope on angel's wings.
Come now and descend
Into this Circle.
In perfect love and perfect trust,
Blessed Goddess,
I invoke Thee!
Welcome!

Lunar Blessings

Under the silver glow of a luminous moon,
We gather in this sacred space,
The blessings of the lunar rite,
We welcome and embrace.

As we dance beneath the stars,
In the moon's guiding light,
We honor its ever-changing cycles,
As it waxes and wanes in the night.

In the new moon's darkness,
We plant our seeds,
Setting goals and intentions,
For what our hearts truly need.

We sow our wishes and our dreams,
From deep within our souls,
Aiding us to manifest our desires,
The lunar energy endlessly unfolds.

As the moon waxes,
we witness its growing light,
A reminder that our own potential

From within, that shines equally bright.

Let us draw down its energy,
To fuel our passions and goals,
Harnessing the power within us,
as it unfolds.

In the Full Moon's radiance,
We bask in its glow,
Illuminating the shadows,
That we've come to know.

We release what no longer serves,
With each exhale,
Creating space for new beginnings,
As we unveil.

When the moon wanes,
It teaches us to let go,
Releasing negativity,
Surrendering to the flow.

In the blessings of the lunar rite,
We find solace and peace,
Connecting to the cycles,
That never ceases.

We honor the moon's ancient wisdom,
in the still of the night,
Embracing the gracious blessings,
On this lunar rite.

The Candle Light Ceremony

[Light the black candle]
I honor and recognize the Great Mother,
Blessed Goddess
She who dwells within
She who is Understanding

Commune with me this night
Welcome!

[Light the white candle]
I honor and recognize the Mighty Father,
Blessed God
He who brought forth Celestial Light
He who is Wisdom
Commune with me this night
Welcome!

[Light the red candle]
I honor and recognize the Solar Lord.
Blessed Son
He who transcended humanity
He who is Beauty and Compassion
Commune with me this night
Welcome!

The Charge of the Goddess

Listen now, my children, to
The words of the Great Mother
Not with your physical ears, but
With your esoteric mind,
For I am the Creatrix of the Universe
She who dwells within,
The spirit that moved upon the waters,
The fountain of hope and dreams.

By many names have I been known:
Asherah, Sophia, Shekinah,
Mother Mary, Mary Magdalene,
Lilith, the Holy Spirit, Anath, Levannah,
Brigid, Zoe, Barbelo, Guadalupe,
And I will be known by many more
For I am the harmony that makes your heart

Beat strong and courageous.
I am the benevolence that brings you to smile
When you think of precious memories.

Whenever you require anything, once a month,
Better when the moon is full, and energy abounds,
Assemble in your sacred place;
Come to your Goddess and
Ask whatever your heart desires.

Lay your fears and wishes at my feet in rest
I am that I am Mother of all living things
I am the Queen of Heaven,
Upon the earth,
I give the presence of the spirit eternal.

I am the flame of gnosis that burns within,
I am the veil between the realms
The Keeper of the Mysteries,
The source of bright beginnings and
The guardian of rainbows and rebirth.
At the end of all things, I will begin again
As all things great and small
Return unto me.

To thou who thinkest to seek Me, know that
Thy seeking and yearning
Shall avail thee not unless thou knowest the Mystery.
If that which thou seekest thou findest not within thee,
Thou wilt never find it without.
For behold,
I have been with you from the beginning, and
I am that which is attained at the end of desire.

Drawing Down the Moon

Now I will
Draw Down the Moon
I raise my hands, beginning to
Feel the Divine essence of the Goddess
As it flows into my fingertips,
Causing warm tingles
Coursing down my arms
Into my body
Igniting my heart and soul.

I hold my hands skyward
To the heavens
To feel your Motherly touch
I invoke Thee
Mighty Mother Goddess of all life:
Earth, Moon, and Waters.

By bud and by seed
By stem and by root
By leaf and by flower and fruit
By life and by love
I invoke Thee to
Descend into this Circle
Into your children
Into the bodies of your
Sons and daughters,
Your priests and priestesses:
Great Lunar Mother
I Invoke Thee!

Blessed be my feet
That has brought me in these ways
[Anoint feet with oil]

Blessed be my knees
That shall kneel at the sacred altar
[Anoint knees with oil]

Blessed be my womb/phallus
Without which, I could not create
[Anoint abdomen with oil]

Blessed be my chest
Formed in beauty/strength
[Anoint chest with oil]

Blessed be my lips
That shall utter the sacred names
[Anoint lips with oil]

[Speak the names aloud]
Anath! Brigid! Zoe!
Barbelo! Shekinah!
Mary Magdalene!
Asherah!
Guadalupe! Sophia!
Lilith! Holy Spirit!
Mother Mary! Levannah!

A Psalm of the Goddess

O Hail to the fair moon,
Our orb of the night
Symbolizing the Great Mother
Who resides in the heavens.
Until the morning light
Beloved Goddess
Shine down on me
Guiding my heart and mind
Like the oceans and tides.

The Moon,

> *She is appointed for seasons:*
> *For when the Sun is going down.*
> *The Sun shall not smite thee by day,*
> *Nor the Moon by night.*
> *Shall we be established forever as the Moon,*
> *And as a faithful witness in the heavens?*
>
> *Blow up the trumpet in the new Moon,*
> *In the time appointed.*
> *The Sun to rule by day,*
> *The Moon and stars by night.*

Magickal Working

Create a Goddess Self-Healing Charm Bag on any full moon. Calling on the Great Mother by a specific name is not necessary for this magickal task. For many, creating this charm bag will be the first craft effort with the Sacred Feminine after disconnecting from the patriarchal Church. For experienced Christopagans, it serves the same purpose: spiritual healing and continuing devotion.

The purpose of this charm bag is to assist the practitioner in embracing our Goddess, healing the wounds created by the denial of the Great Mother, and surrounding yourself with Her nurturing energy.

> 1 Attractive Pink 2" x 3" cotton or hobby bag
> 1 Pink Chime Candle
> Vanilla Fragrance Oil

Choose any nine symbols associated with the Goddess for your charm bag. Add any Goddess items that resonate with you. For example, a pearl, rose petal, or dried bud, a symbol of the moon, pink quartz, a seashell, a heart, a dove, a spiral, salt, a star, or a piece of silver.

Place your chosen objects into the pink bag and tighten the strings. Anoint your charm bag and the pink chime candle with vanilla oil. Light the candle and place the charm bag next to it. Chime candles can burn for 20 to 90 minutes. Write your own affirmation or speak the following:

With this pearl, I reclaim the forgotten Goddess
With this rose, I acknowledge my inner beauty
With this moon, I embrace Her enlightenment
With this salt, I declare my quest for wisdom
With this dove, I find inner peace,
With this heart, I am imbued with self-love,
With this star, I believe in Divine hope,
With this sea shell, I acknowledge the waters of rebirth
With this spiral, I enter the dimension of the Great Mother.
So as I will it, so mote it be!
Blessed Be!

Raising & Releasing Energy

As above, So below
Between my hands
I feel the energy grow!
To shape, mold, and create
Only that which I can facilitate.
The Circle Within Me

And the Circle Without
Never Ending Power Endowed
And for a few wondrous moments
I am Ancient Power

I now release this Lunar Energy!
So as I will it, So mote it be:
Release!

The Great Rite

Candle to candle,
Spirit to the flesh, male to female
Divine Husband to Divine Wife
I celebrate the Sacred Union of
My God and Goddess
Divine Beings,
Creators of all living things
The image of all human life.

[Lights the outer two candles; then take those two candles
and together light the third candle in the middle]

Feast and Libations

[Hold up the plate of cakes toward the heavens and say:]
On this night, this Lunar rite,
I celebrate the Goddess
And share these cakes, symbolic of the
Grains that sustain my body:
I partake so that I may never hunger.

[Put a portion of the food on a separate plate
as a sign of thanks and communion.]

[Raise a chalice of wine or juice towards the heavens and say:]
On this night, this Lunar rite,
I celebrate the Goddess
And share this drink of the vine,

Symbolic of the blood of life:
I partake so that I may never thirst.
Blessed Be!

[Pour a portion of the wine onto the ground.]

Journal Your Thoughts

Thank the Deities

I thank the Goddess,
The Great Mother and Queen of Heaven
For being with me and empowering me,
On this Lunar Rite.

I acknowledge the Blessed Trinity:
Always with me, the Divine spark within
Forever guiding me on
My spiritual journey
Stay if you will; go if you must
In Perfect Love and Perfect Trust!
Blessed Be!

Dismiss the Quarters

I thank the Guardians of the Watchtowers
Of the North,
For being with me
This night, this lunar rite
Stay if you will; go if you must
Hail and Farewell!

I thank the Guardians of the Watchtowers
Of the West,
For being with me
This night, this lunar rite
Stay if you will; go if you must

Hail and Farewell!

I thank the Guardians of the Watchtowers
Of the South,
For being with me
This night, this lunar rite
Stay if you will; go if you must
Hail and Farewell!

I thank the Guardians of the Watchtowers
Of the East
For being with me
This Night, this lunar rite
Stay if you will; go if you must
Hail and Farewell!

Dismiss the Circle

This Lunar rite is now ended
The beloved Goddess has been honored
I have felt Her loving touch,
Tonight Great Mother,
I ask you to dwell with me always!

The Circle is open but never broken
May the peace of the Trinity
Be ever in your heart:
So, Merry we meet, and merry we part
'Til merry we meet again!
Blessed Be!

Sabbats

The Sabbats are the eight annual solar festivals that align with the equinoxes, solstices, and midway points, occurring approximately every 6 weeks. They are traditionally categorized into two groups based on the Sun's relationship with the Earth. The greater Sabbats, also known as the cross-quarter Sabbats, are celebrated at the peak of each season. These Sabbats are influenced by the Celtic fire festivals: Imbolc, Beltane, Lammas, and Samhain.

The lesser Sabbats or the quarter Sabbats mark the beginning of each season. They are represented by the solstices and the equinoxes: Yule, Ostara, Litha, and Mabon. While the cardinal point Sabbats can be found in various indigenous practices worldwide, the lesser Sabbats in Wicca are attributed to Germanic traditions.

Samhain (October 31st): Also known as the Witches' New Year, Samhain celebrates the conclusion of the harvest season and the commencement of the dark half of the year. It is a time to honor and communicate with ancestors, contemplate our mortality, and celebrate the thinning of the veil between the physical and spiritual realms.

Yule (December 21st): Celebrated around the winter solstice, Yule is a festival of light and rebirth. It marks the shortest day and longest night of the year, symbolizing the return of the sun and the promise of new beginnings. This festival encourages self-reflection, rejuvenation, and celebrating the return of light.

Candlemas (February 2nd): Also known as Imbolc, heralds the arrival of Spring and the awakening of the Earth. It is associated with Brigid and Mother Mary as a time for purification, inspiration, and new growth. It is celebrated by lighting candles, making Brigid's crosses and corn dollies, and performing rituals celebrating home and hearth.

Ostara (March 20th): On the Spring Equinox, this festival celebrates the balance of light and dark as the days become longer. It is a time of fertility, renewal, and new beginnings. It is associated with the Goddess

Zoe and is often celebrated with rituals involving eggs, flowers, and the planting of seeds.

Beltane (May 1st): Beltane marks the beginning of summer and celebrates fertility, passion, and abundance. It is associated with the union of the god and goddess, symbolizing the blossoming of life and the Earth's vitality. It is celebrated with bonfires, dancing, and rituals to honor the Sacred Union of the Divine Feminine and the Divine Masculine.

Litha (June 21st): Also known as MidSummer, occurs on the Summer Solstice. It is the longest day and shortest night of the year. It celebrates the peak of the Sun's power and the abundance of nature. It is a time to honor our Solar Lord Jesus, embrace the season's energy, and celebrate growth and manifestation.

Lammas (August 1st): Also known as Lughnasadh, this marks the beginning of the harvest season. It is a time to give thanks for the Earth's abundance and the voluntary self-sacrifice of our Solar Lord to enrich the harvest. It is associated with the first yield and illustrates the cycle of life, death, and rebirth.

Mabon (September 21st): On the Autumn Equinox, Mabon is a time of balance between light and dark hours as the days grow shorter. It is a time to give thanks for the harvest, to reflect on the balance in our lives, and to prepare for winter's approach. The festivities are celebrated with plentiful feasts, heartfelt rituals of gratitude, and the sharing of the harvest bounty.

Sabbats are not merely about interacting with the Elohian deities throughout the year. While they are a means of getting back in touch with nature and learning the lessons the seasons teach, sabbats are instrumental for us to heal and grow spiritually by reuniting our deeply fractured selves. Regardless of our outward gender, we are each both male and female inwardly. By awakening the Divine Feminine and acknowledging the true Divine Masculine, humanity can restore the imbalances created by patriarchal societies prior to the onset of the Church.

Sabbats are meant to be honored more than one day every 6 weeks. The time leading up to each sabbat should be approached much like secular holidays are observed–as a holiday season. A good rule of thumb is to give yourself three days of rest before preparing for the next sabbat. Then begin changes to the sabbat decorations in your home, incense, and candle colors. Exchange their ornaments if you keep a sabbat wreath on your front door.

Kyriats

In Trinitarian Wicca, Jesus is revered as the Solar Lord and is honored during the lesser sabbats: the equinoxes and solstices, which we call Kyriats. The term was coined for this tradition but is derived from the Greek *"Kyrie Eleison."* This phrase can be found in Psalm 123:3: *Have mercy upon us, O Lord, have mercy upon us: for we are exceedingly filled with contempt.*

Trinitarian Wicca celebrates the Kyriats as solar festivals that honor Jesus as the Solar Lord and his annual journey as the Dying and Rising God. Kyriats are determined by the position of the Sun in relation to the Earth, creating the seasons for planting, growing, harvesting, and laying fallow. The amount of light, not only the Sun's heat, directs the theme of the sabbat.

Yule, or Winter Solstice, is the Kyriat of Rebirth.
Ostara, or Spring Equinox, is the Kyriat of the Pilgrimage.
Midsummer, or Summer Solstice, is the Kyriat of Initiation.
Mabon, or Autumn Equinox, is the Kyriat of the Feast.

There are a few minor differences between the ritual parts of the Sabbats and Kyriats. Kyriats invoke the Elohim, or the GodPair, instead of the Blessed Trinity. Because the emphasis is on the Solar Lord, Kyriats focus on the parallels of the sun's position as it pertains to the life of the Biblical Jesus.

Blessed Be the Trinity acknowledges the Social Trinity in three parts, including their individual characteristics and distinct personalities, with a special salutation to the Solar Lord with the phrase *"Kyrie Eleison: Lord [Jesus] have mercy."*

The Kyriats have been renamed from the original 2003 book. I realized something significant was missing from how the lesser sabbat rituals were observed by open Circles and overlooked in Wicca for Beginner-styled books. I saw the pattern forming, but without a solid background in mythology, my studies hadn't led me to the correct sources to best express my thoughts.

James G. Frazer's influential work, *The Golden Bough*, published in 1890, was the first to bring the idea into comparative mythology. It outlines the recurring cycle of birth, life, death, and rebirth of young male fertility gods in the Mediterranean in association with a virgin mother. Many of these deities were born to kingship in agrarian societies and met similar obstacles. As it is linked to the recurring seasonal cycles of nature, it is ideal to emphasize it in Wicca.

This concept is not exclusive to any one belief system. It can be found in various forms across different cultures and religions. It is a common theme found in many religious narratives. Examples of the Dying and Rising Gods include Osiris, Tammuz, Adonis and Attis, Zagreus, Dionysus, and Jesus. The drama of their journey, obstacles, and destinies is filled with life lessons. Their followers have created and performed melodramas as part of initiation ceremonies and commemorative rituals.

Joseph Campbell's *Hero's Journey* is a masterful work examining these reoccurring patterns in mythology. Trinitarian Wicca uses the three-stage Hero's Journey framework to further understand the symbolism of Jesus, the Solar Lord, as the Rising and Dying God's correlation to the solstices and equinoxes. The three-stage motif is Departure, Initiation, and Return.

Ostara is the Departure stage aligning with the energies of Spring Equinox, symbolizing new beginnings and rebirth. This is when the Hero receives their Call to Adventure and leaves his ordinary life to step into an extraordinary one.

Litha is the Initiation stage aligning with the energies of the Summer Solstice, which is a time of fullness and abundance. Our Solar Lord is at the height of His power, facing trials and challenges that require him to commit himself to his new role—this is his point of no return.

Mabon is the Return stage aligning with the energies of the Autumn Equinox, a time of balance and reflection. This symbolizes when the Solar Hero comes back to their ordinary world, transformed by his experiences, sharing his newly acquired wisdom with the community.

Yule aligns with the Winter Solstice, representing the birth/rebirth of the Sun. This is the Solar Hero's rebirth after his journey, and the cycle begins again.

The Hero's Journey, or the monomyth, is a timeless, universal narrative pattern found in mythology and folklore from different cultures worldwide. It is based on perennial themes such as courage, sacrifice, and the search for truth.

The monomyth has universal appeal, resonating with people from different cultures and backgrounds because it deals with familiar aspects of life. This universal story conveys ideas such as self-discovery, overcoming obstacles, and transformation, which can be related to regardless of one's location or background.

The Hero's Journey typically involves a central character who faces trials, temptations, and failures and eventually triumphs over adversity. This narrative creates an emotional bond between the reader/viewer and the hero, as they cheer for his success and empathize with their struggles.

The monomyth is known for its iconic archetypal characters: the hero, mentor, threshold guardian, and villain. These characters embody universal traits and roles, making them easily recognizable and relatable to the audience. These highly familiar figures help create stories that are memorable and lasting.

Yule: The Kyriat of Rebirth
December 22

Ritual Correspondences

Altar cloth: green or red
Candles: green, white, and red
Herbs: cinnamon sticks, cloves, nutmeg
Stones: ruby, garnet, green tourmaline, and clear quartz
Observances: Lighting the Yule Log or decorating a small evergreen
Decorations: seasonal greenery, wreaths, pinecones
Sabbat mythos: The birth of the Solar Lord
Sun position: 0 degrees Capricorn
Tarot Card: The Sun
Rune: Sowilo
Angel: Gabriel

Yule, a joyous celebration of light and rebirth, is observed by cultures worldwide as the Winter Solstice. This sacred festival marks the shortest day and longest night of the year, symbolizing the victory of light over darkness. It serves as a turning point to indicate longer days ahead and the anticipation of spring. Yule represents renewal, introducing warmth and light that brings hope and joy to illuminate the dark part of the year.

This sabbat celebrates the return of the youthful Solar Lord. Having rested in the Underworld, the Aging God's spirit visits his Snow Queen one final time, witnessing His rebirth. Joy and delight fill her heart as she beholds her Beloved Consort while cries from her Promised Child fill the air. The Solar Lord's return symbolizes the emergence of sunlight and warmth.

Yule is a time of joy and celebration. People typically light candles, ignite bonfires, and drape their homes with strings of lights. The theme resonates deeply with humanity as light represents positivity, expectation, warmth, and life. Yule reminds us of life's cyclical nature, the significance of hope, and gathering with loved ones to share meals and gifts. The Yule feast on Winter Solstice reminds us to reflect upon our blessings from the past year and look forward to new beginnings. Other traditional customs include decorating or constructing Yule Logs or trees; these serve as a reminder to keep traditions alive throughout the year.

Some practice traditional rituals such as wassailing, which involves singing songs of goodwill while visiting neighbors' homes or drinking cider made from specially harvested apples. These practices bring cheer while ushering in better days.

Yule Midnight Meditation

Yule Eve marks the longest night of the year for profound contemplation and meditation. This is a sacred night for seeking stillness to move forward with clarity and purpose. It is a unique opportunity to connect with the dark mysteries of the winter solstice to receive guidance from worlds beyond our own. This is a time to nurture your soul with restful peace.

Prepare yourself with rituals that draw upon ancient and modern Yule traditions. Gather evergreens, light candles, burn incense, hang stars in your window, create an altar, meditate on symbols such as snowflakes or reindeer – anything that resonates with your spirit. Allow yourself to enter deep self-reflection, connecting with your inner wisdom and Divinity.

Find a tranquil spot where you can either sit or lie down. Adjust the lights to create a calming atmosphere, or flicker a candle. Take some deep breaths and allow your body and mind to rest. Picture yourself in a wintery scene of nature, feeling the chill of the air and savoring the tranquility of nightfall.

As you breathe, imagine that you're inhaling the mysterious energy of darkness and letting it enfold you. Release any worry as you exhale.

Allow the dark to refresh and purify your being. Shift your awareness towards your heart center and envision a flame burning inside your chest – an essence of light and optimism. Watch this ember grow brighter and stronger with each breath until it spreads warmth throughout your body.

Reflect on all that has occurred this past year: what lessons have been acquired, and what obstacles have been overcome? Give thanks for personal growth and strength. Set intentions for the coming year and ambitions to manifest or cultivate in your life. Spend time in reflection and openness to insight arising from the night's silence. When ready, bring your awareness back to the present by wiggling your fingers and toes and slowly opening your eyes.

As you gaze out into the darkness, let it remind you that although we may feel lost sometimes, we must trust ourselves and the journey ahead. Embrace this Yule season as one of renewal, awakening from darkness into light, knowing that whatever comes our way has great potential for transformation.

Consecrate the Area

[Add a pinch of salt to the bowl of water and hold it
toward the sky, asking this or similar blessings:]

I call upon the Blessed Trinity to
Consecrate this water and this salt for the
Elemental Purification of this Circle.
Representing my Goddess:
Of the Earth and Water of the Sea,
So as I will it, So mote it be!

[Using the flame of a candle, light the incense,
and hold it toward the sky,
asking this or similar blessings:]

I call upon the Blessed Trinity to
Consecrate this flame and
This incense for the
Elemental Purification of this Circle.

Representing my God:
By Fire and Air, Glory to Thee
So as I will it, So mote It Be!

Elemental Chant

[Chant as you consecrate the Circle:]

Earth, my body;
Water my blood.
Air my breath; and
Fire my spirit.

Cast the Circle

I summon this Circle
Three times three
A perfect sphere of harmony
With earthly vibrations of energy
This joyous day, I celebrate Yule
So, As I will it, So Mote it Be!

Call the Quarters

Hail to the Archangel Raphael
Guardian of the Watchtowers of the East
Messenger of the Divine
Keeper of the element of Air
As I Follow the Flaming Star of Gnosis
Bless me this Kyriat of Rebirth:
I Invoke Thee!
Welcome!

Hail to the Archangel Michael
Guardian of the Watchtowers of the South
Messenger of the Divine
Keeper of the element of Fire

As I Follow the Flaming Star of Gnosis
Bless me this Kyriat of Rebirth:
I invoke Thee!
Welcome!

Hail to the Archangel Gabriel
Guardian of the Watchtowers of the West
Messenger of the Divine
Keeper of Water and Intuition
As I Follow the Flaming Star of Gnosis
Bless me this Kyriat of Rebirth:
I invoke Thee!
Welcome!

Hail to the Archangel Uriel
Guardian of the Watchtowers of the North
Messenger of the Divine
Keeper of the element of Earth
As I Follow the Flaming Star of Gnosis
Bless me this Kyriat of Rebirth:
I invoke Thee!
Welcome!

Invocation of the Elohim

Hail to the Glorious Lord and Lady
Guardians of the Celestial Realm
Rulers of the Sun and Moon
Sovereign engineers of the Constellations
Descend from the heavens and assemble here
Be with me to experience the
Magick and the Mysteries
Of this Yule Rite.

The Kyriat of Rebirth
Acknowledges the return of
The Promised Sun,
After dwelling for three days

In the Stellar Underworld
At the Southern Cross.

The Light of the World
Solar savior of the age
Lord of Lords, King of Kings
Lover, Provider, and Sage
May your power be Evergreen!
Hosts of the Almighty Elohim
Welcome!
I invoke thee!
Blessed Be the Elohim!

The Spirit of Yule

In the depths of Winter's embrace,
We gather near the hearth,
To celebrate the blessings of Yule,
A time of rebirth.
As the sun stands still in the sky,
Casting its faintest light,
We honor the ancient wisdom
That guides us through the night.

The earth lies dormant,
Covered in a blanket of snow,
Yet beneath the frozen surface,
Life continues to grow.
In this season of darkness,
We find solace and peace,
Embracing the stillness
As our worries cease.

Amid the longest night,
The air is filled with cheer,
As we welcome the return of the Sun,
Drawing ever near.
As the sun begins its ascent,

Stretching its rays from afar,
We feel the warmth of its embrace,
Like a Guiding Star.

So, let us find strength and renewal
As the Yule Log burns,
May the blessings of Yule fill our hearts
With the magic of this sacred turn.

The Goddess Speaks

Merry Meet, Traveler
The wheel has turned on and
Yule is upon us.
I am the aging Snow Queen,
Heavy with child;
Winter Solstice brings the
Birth of the Child of Promise.

With the Oak King,
Comes strength and renewal
As Father Time, the fallen Holly King
Ascends one last time from the Underworld
Passing his all-encompassing power.

At the time of His celestial birth,
I will transform once again into
The Youthful Maiden.

This a time of mystic transformation
As the essence of the Old Lord is crowned renewed
On the Glorious Babe of Future Light
Signaling the Return of the
Sol Invictus,
The Unconquered Sun.

Blessings of Yule to you,
Dear Traveler

May the grace of this sabbat
Bring regeneration and hope
On this ongoing
Journey in this World and
In the Next: Blessed Be!

Lighting the Seasonal Candles

[Lighting of the White Candle]
Blessed Be the Season of Yule
Blessed is Mother Mary
Earthly Mother of the Solar Lord Jesus
On this day, I Celebrate!

On this Winter's Solstice
Assembling in the cold and quiet,
I give thanks for this Winterland of enchantment
On this Longest Night of the Year!

Nurturing Goddess, Compassionate God
I thank you for
For the many blessings of Yule,
And all this season stands for:
I celebrate and sing praises!
Joy to the heavens on high!

I sing and dance a carol,
And a-wassailing, I go
The Yule log burns bright,
On this Winter's Night, with smiles all a-glow
I sing and dance a carol
With the Hope of Winter's Snow.

[Lighting of the Green Candle]
Season's blessings I ask for Yule
This day, Winter Solstice.
I sing, and dance and merry make
Celebrate this Christmas time.
Apples, oranges, and lemons:
Nature now decorates my door and boughs
My tree is brightly lit to show
My rejoicing and my vows.

The Fresh Evergreens brings harmony.
December's magick and mistletoe
The holly and the ivy
Sets my heart a-glow.
The greenery is a promise that
Spring will soon reappear
So I will make joy and melody tonight
And in my heart throughout the year!

[The Lighting of the Red Candle]
Season's Tidings: I bid this Yule
As the Sun's ascent begins its rule
As I sing and praise merrily,
Dancing around the Holly and Oak Tree

Joy, peace, and giving are key
To a light and happy heart's decree.
Love within and Love without
God, Goddess, and Solar Lord spread about
There is a message: if I lend an ear
A story I open my heart to hear
Faith, hope, and love are shed from the light

I raise my hand to praise the delight
As it grows to heat the frozen lands
The love of this season is Evergreen

The Kyriat of Rebirth

Winter Solstice, the Sun
Sinks lower in the sky from our sight
It appears to end its cosmic journey
At the Southern Cross.

There it remains for three days,
Before the Sun reverses course
As if returning
From the celestial Underground.

The heights of Enlightenment
Are limitless, and
Awareness is the key.
I will continue to excel
The limitations of the flesh.
The Oral Teachings of the Mysteries
Lie hidden with me,
Reoccurring in every age.

The miracle nature promises with
The birth of the Solar Lord as
The process of life begins again.
Nothing ever truly dies or fades away:
We are ultimately pure energy,
The essence of the heavens and
The Earth combined.
As above, so below.

Blessed Be the Trinity

Blessed be the God

Kyrie Eleison!
Blessed be the Goddess
Kyrie Eleison!
Blessed be the Solar Lord
Kyrie Eleison!

Blessings to the God
King of the heavens and cosmos
Father of sustenance and power
Our God of infinite existence

Blessings to the Goddess
Queen of the Earth and Seas
Mother of creation and fortitude
Our Goddess of infinite existence

Blessings to the Solar Son
Prince of peace and love
Son of sacrifice and selflessness
Our Solar Lord of infinite existence

Blessed Be the Trinity
This Kyriat of Rebirth
Kyrie Eleison, Kyrie Eleison
Kyrie Eleison!

The Lighting of the Yule Log

[Lighting the first wick]
Faith is the reason for the season
[Lighting the second wick]
Hope is the dream and desire
[Lighting the third wick]
Love is the Mystical Fire

Three Wicks are lit,
Three wishes set free:
Faith, Hope, and Love
So mote it be!

Raising & Releasing Energy

As above, so below
Between my hands
I feel the energy grow...
To shape, mold, and create
Only I can facilitate.

The Circle within me
And the Circle without
Neverending power endowed
And for a few wondrous moments

I now release this energy of Yule!
So as I will it, So mote it be:
Release!

The Great Rite

As the Spear to the Cauldron,
The Lance to the Grail
Spirit to Flesh,
The Cakes and the Ale

The Alchemical Wedding
Unites the Lady and Lord;
Love makes One from Two
The Chalice and the Sword.

Feast and Libations

[Hold up the plate of cakes toward the heavens and say]
On this joyous day of Yule, I celebrate
And share these cakes, symbolic of the
Grains that sustain my body:
I partake so that I may never hunger.

[Put a portion of the food on a separate plate
as a sign of thanks and communion.]

[Raise a chalice of wine or juice towards the heavens and say:]
On this joyous day of Yule, I celebrate
And share this drink of the vine,
Symbolic of the blood of life:
I partake so that I may never thirst.
Blessed Be!

[Pour a portion of the wine onto the ground.]

Journal Your Thoughts

Thank the Deities

As this ritual of Yule draws to a close,
I honor the Elohian pantheon:
My wondrous Goddess, my mighty God, and
My Solar Lord, Jesus.
Thank you for witnessing this Solar Rite
As you continue to bestow your essence of
Life, love, and renewal each day.
Blessed Be the Trinity!

Dismiss the Quarters

Archangel Uriel
Guardian of the Watchtowers of the North
Messenger of Earth
I thank you for being with me
This Kyriat of the rebirth
Stay if you will; go if you must
Hail and Farewell!

Archangel Gabriel
Guardian of the Watchtowers of the West

Messenger of Water
I thank you for being with me
This Kyriat of the rebirth
Stay if you will; go if you must
Hail and Farewell!

Archangel Michael
Guardian of the Watchtowers of the South
Messenger of Fire
I thank you for being with me
This Kyriat of the rebirth
Stay if you will; go if you must
Hail and Farewell!

Archangel Raphael
Guardian of the Watchtowers of the East
Messenger of Air
I thank you for being with me
This Kyriat of the rebirth
Stay if you will; go if you must
Hail and Farewell!

Dismiss the Circle

This Rite of Yule has now ended;
The Wheel of the Year turns on…
I have celebrated the rebirth of
The Solar Lord, Jesus, as
The path of the Sun now returns.

This Circle is open but never broken.
May the peace of the Trinity
Be ever in your heart.
Merry we meet, and merry we part,
'til merry, we meet again!
Blessed Be!

145

Candlemas or Imbolc
February 2nd

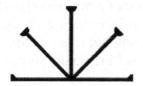

Ritual Correspondences

Altar cloth: white
Candles: yellow, white, pink
Herbs: chamomile, rose hips, sage
Stones: amber, carnelian, citrine, clear, and rose quartz
Observances: Create a wreath of white candles for the center of the altar
Decorations: candles, candle wreaths, corn dollies, sun wheels
Sabbat Mythos: Purification of the Goddess, becoming a Maiden,
As the Sun Child grows strong
Sun position: Sun in 15 degrees Aquarius
Tarot Card: The Priestess
Rune: Berkana
Angel: Uriel

The festival of Candlemas, also called Imbolc or St. Brigid's Day, is a solar festival celebrated on February 2nd as the transition from winter to springtime. This holiday marks the first stage of budding life stirring in nature as the daylight hours grow each day. Candlemas, called the Festival of Light, uses candles and bonfires to encourage the return of the Sun's light and warmth.

Derived from ancient Celtic traditions, this holiday is the midpoint between the Winter Solstice and the Spring Equinox. Candlemas is a ritual of fire and purification, cleansing lifeless residual energies that can build up during Winter. Although Candlemas is a solar festival, its energy is feminine. Brigid is the Celtic goddess of fertility, creativity, healing, and poetry.

Making a candle wreath to crown the priestess' head is a beautiful tradition. However, I suggest making the wreath for your altar using white candles for safety. The fire's glow is meant to signify spiritual knowledge or gnosis. The Early Church Fathers incorporated the mystery of Fire in the Head by including a halo in their artwork. This halo-shaped candle formation was meant to represent the uniting of Celtic culture and the Greco-Roman Mysteries as Christianity spread.

Another tradition is making Brigid's Cross, woven from rushes or straw, and hung in homes for protection and good luck. You can also create Brigid's bed. Assembling a small bed for the Goddess, adorned with food and drink offerings, is believed to ensure Brigid's blessings and a prosperous year.

One of Brigid's aspects is the bride, a symbol of fertility, prosperity, and a reminder of the cycle of life, death, and rebirth. Her doll is made of woven corn husks. If you make a corn doll at Lammas, you can dress it in the colors for Candlemas.

Additional symbols associated with this sabbat include snowdrops, which celebrate the triumph of life over death; lambs, which signify innocence and purity; and robins, which represent the courage to take on new challenges.

Consecrate the Area

[Add a pinch of salt to the bowl of water and hold it toward the sky, asking this or similar blessings:]

I call upon the Blessed Trinity to

Consecrate this water and this salt for the
Elemental Purification of this Circle.
Representing my Goddess:
Of the Earth and Water of the Sea —
So as I will it, So mote it be!

[Using the flame of a candle, light the incense,
and hold it toward the sky,
asking this or similar blessings:]

I call upon the Blessed Trinity to
Consecrate this flame and
This incense for the
Elemental Purification of this Circle.
Representing my God:
By Fire and Air, Glory to Thee
So as I will it, So mote It Be!

Elemental Chant

[Chant as you consecrate the Circle:]

Earth, my body;
Water my blood.
Air my breath; and
Fire my spirit.

Prelude

In the beginning, Elohim created the heavens and the Earth.
And the earth was without form and void and darkness
Moved upon the face of the deep!

And the Shekinah moved upon the face of the waters.
And the Elohim said, Let there be light:
And there was Light.

[Light the altar and quarter candles clockwise, starting in the east.

Light the white candles on the wreath.]

Cast the Circle

I call upon the Ancient Forces
To form and shape this Circle.
Aid me to assemble this Sacred Space
On this joyous day,
I celebrate Candlemas.
So as I Will it, So mote it Be!

Call the Quarters

O Divine Guardians of Light
Ancient and Mighty Ones of the East
Keepers of Air and Intelligence
Lend Me Your Power and Glory
Protect Me this Night of Candlemas
I Invoke thee this Night:
Our Festival of Lights
Welcome!

O Divine Guardians of Light
Ancient and Mighty Ones of the South
Keepers of Fire and Strength
Lend Me Your Power and Glory
Protect Me this Night of Candlemas
I Invoke thee this Night:
Our Festival of Lights
Welcome!

O Divine Guardians of Light
Ancient and Mighty Ones of the West
Keepers of Water and Clairvoyance
Lend Me Your Power and Glory
Protect Me this Night of Candlemas
I Invoke thee this Night:

Our Festival of Lights
Welcome!

O Divine Guardians of Light
Ancient and Mighty Ones of the North
Keepers of Earth and Stability
Lend Me Your Power and Glory
Protect Me this Night of Candlemas
I Invoke thee this Night:
Our Festival of Lights
Welcome!

Invocation of the Blessed Trinity

Blessed Be this day of Candlemas
To Honor the Maiden Goddess and
Urge the return of the Sun
I invoke the Blessed Trinity:

Sacred Mother, Queen of the Earth and Seas
Mother of creation and life
Our Goddess of infinite existence

Divine Father, King of the Heavens and Cosmos
Father of sustenance and power
Our God of endless presence

Solar Lord, Prince of Peace and Charity
Son of sacrifice and selfless love
Our Solar Lord of radiant immortality:
Be with me to experience the
Magick and the Mysteries
In this Rite of Candlemas
I Invoke Thee:
Welcome!

The Blessings of Candlemas

Candlemas is the festival of light and hope,
To honor the returning Sun when days are still short.
Amid the Winter's darkness,
One by one, we light the candles
Inviting the blessings of the returning Sun.

Candlemas, a time of purification and renewal,
To honor the Divine Feminine,
Acknowledging forgotten wisdom and
Our strength from within.

We pay homage to Brigid, the goddess of Sacred Fire,
Who's healing touch ignites\our passions and desires.
We recognize Mother Mary, the goddess of Fortitude,
Who gave birth to the Solar Lord,
We express our gratitude.

As the days grow longer and the Sun returns,
We feel the energy shift,
As the Wheel of the Year turns.
With each passing day, we step into the light,
guided by a greater force with our hearts open wide,
May the blessings of Candlemas fill our souls and our days,
As we journey onward in love and praise.

The Goddess Speaks

Merry Meet Traveler,
On this day, we celebrate the return
Of the Sun, warming the Earth
And my purification,
I am a Young Maiden again,
First Golden ray of the Sun peeks
Shyly through the gray clouds.

It is now midwinter, and

Our young Solar Lord
Makes His ever-increasing presence
Known with each day.
My children light candles and
Bonfires to encourage Him
To grow to His
Full potential.

Dear Traveler
I wish you all the blessings
Of Candlemas.
May the grace of this sabbat
Bring light and renewal as you
Journey in this world and the next:
Blessed Be!

Purification by the Elements

[Light the Altar Candle]
In the Spirit of Purification
On this Rite of Candlemas:
I offer this Symbol of Fire.
Blessed Be!

[Light the Altar Incense]
In the Spirit of Purification
On this Rite of Candlemas:
I offer this Symbol of Air
Blessed Be!

[Sprinkle the Dirt or Sand on the Altar]
In the Spirit of Purification
On this Rite of Candlemas:
I offer this Symbol of Earth
Blessed Be!

[Sprinkle Water on the Altar]
In the Spirit of Purification
On this Rite of Candlemas:

I offer this Symbol of Water
Blessed Be!

[Toss a Sprig of Evergreen into the Fire,
preferably from the Yule Tree]
As this Symbol of Winter Is Consumed by the Fire,
So Is the Darkness Consumed by the Light!

Raising & Releasing Energy

As above, so below
Between my hands
I feel the energy grow!

To shape, mold, and create
Which only I can facilitate
The Circle Within and
The Circle Without
Never-ending energy capable of
Magick and Miracles
From which all things
May be obtained:
So as I will it, So mote it be!

I now release this Energy of Candlemas!

The Great Rite

As the Spear to the Cauldron,
The Lance to the Grail
Spirit to Flesh,
The Cakes and the Ale

The Alchemical Wedding
Unites the Lady and Lord;
Love makes One from Two
The Chalice and the Sword.

Feast and Libations

[Hold up the plate of cakes toward the heavens and say:]
On this magickal day of Candlemas, I celebrate
And share these cakes, symbolic of the
Grains that sustain my body:
I partake so that I may never hunger.

[Put a portion of the food on a separate plate
as a sign of thanks and communion.]

[Raise a chalice of wine or juice towards the heavens and say:]
On this magickal day of Candlemas, I celebrate
And share this drink of the vine,
Symbolic of the blood of life:
I partake so that I may never thirst.
Blessed Be!

[Pour a portion of the wine onto the ground.]

Journal Your Thoughts

Thank the Deities

As this ritual of Candlemas draws to a close,
I honor the Elohian Pantheon:
The wondrous Goddess, mighty God, and
Solar Lord Jesus.
Thank you for witnessing this Solar Rite
As you continue to bestow your essence of
Life, love, and renewal each day.
Blessed Be the Trinity!

Dismiss the Quarters

I wish to thank the
Divine Guardians of Light

Powers of the North
For being with me
This rite of Candlemas
Stay if you will; go if you must
Hail and Farewell!

I wish to thank the
Divine Guardians of Light
Powers of the West
For being with me
This rite of Candlemas
Stay if you will; go if you must
Hail and Farewell!

I wish to thank the
Divine Guardians of Light
Powers of the South
For being with me
This Rite of Candlemas
Stay if you will; go if you must
Hail and Farewell!

I wish to thank the
Divine Guardians of Light
Powers of the East
For being with me
This Rite of Candlemas
Stay if you will; go if you must
Hail and Farewell!

Dismiss the Circle

The Rite of Candlemas has now ended
The Maiden Mother and the
Promised Child has been honored
As the fires of purification
Guide the return of the Sun!

This Circle is open but never broken.
May the peace of the Trinity
Be ever in your heart.
Merry we meet, and merry we part,
'til merry, we meet again!
Blessed Be!

Ostara: The Kyriat of Pilgrimage
March 21

Ritual Correspondences

Altar cloth: pastel green
Candles: white, pastel green, and yellow
Herbs: marjoram, thyme, jasmine, roses, violets
Stones: pink or green tourmaline, rose, and clear quartz
Observances: Fertility with seeds, a potted plant, and decorated eggs
Decorations: bulb flowers of the season: tulips, irises, lilies, jonquils
Sabbat Mythos: The Divine Child has grown, and the Goddess is a
maiden.
Sun position: Sun is at 0 degrees Aries
Tarot Card: The Fool
Rune: Jera
Angel: Raphael

Ostara is celebrated at the Spring Equinox, the first day of Spring. The long-awaited end of winter has finally come, and the sun grows in intensity. Ostara marks the rebirth and renewal of nature when plants start to sprout, flowers bloom, and animals awaken from hibernation.

Ostara is when day and night are equal in length. This represents the balance between light and darkness and the transition from the dark winter months to the brighter days of Spring.

The cosmic egg is a concept in mythology that explains the origins of the universe. The egg symbolizes the duality of nature: the yolk and white, the spirit and the matter, the masculine and the feminine, that together bring life into existence. The cosmic egg is a reminder that life is a grand

and mysterious adventure and that the universe continues to hold many secrets waiting to be discovered.

The Solar Lord has flourished and enters his first sabbat as a virile, passionate male. Our Hero begins the departure stage of his journey.

Despite being the first day of Spring and the celebration of the return of the warmth and light of the Sun, I have found that several traditions do not put as much emphasis on Ostara as the other sabbats. It has been called "a holy gardening day" and referred to as only a seasonal marker. But every sabbat is what you make of it.

Sunrise Ostara Meditation

This guided meditation is for Trinitarian Wiccans to celebrate the arrival of Ostara with an early morning meditation, much like sunrise services performed on Easter morning. As the sun rises, allow yourself to connect with the energy of the new season, focusing on the themes of rebirth, renewal, and balance. Find a comfortable position, relaxed but keeping your spine straight. Close your eyes and take a few deep breaths, inhaling through your nose and exhaling through your mouth.

Visualize roots growing from the base of your spine, reaching deep into the earth. Feel the earth's grounding energy flowing upward, filling your body with stability and strength. Allow this energy to center and prepare you for your meditation.

Imagine standing in a beautiful meadow, surrounded by Spring's blooming flowers and lush greenery. The sky is painted with pink, orange, and gold hues as the sun rises. Feel the gentle warmth of the sun's rays on your skin, filling you with joy and anticipation.

Visualize the four elements surrounding you. Begin with earth, feeling the solid ground beneath your feet and its stability. Move on to air, feeling a gentle breeze brushing against your skin, carrying the scents of spring. Embrace the warmth of fire as the Sun's rays energize and ignite your inner flame. Finally, connect with water, sensing the flow of life and emotions within you.

As the sun rises, imagine a beam of golden light descending from the sky, enveloping you in its warmth. Feel this light penetrating every cell of your being, cleansing and rejuvenating you. Visualize any stagnant energy or negativity released, making space for new beginnings and growth.

With the arrival of Ostara, the day and night are in perfect balance. Reflect on the importance of balance in your life. Visualize a scale, with one side representing your physical aspects and the other representing your spiritual aspects. Observe the balance between these two aspects, ensuring neither side outweighs the other. Embrace the harmony and equilibrium within yourself.

As the meditation comes to a close, take a moment to set your intentions for the coming season. What do you wish to manifest and cultivate in your life? Visualize these intentions as seeds planted in your mind's fertile soil, ready to grow and blossom throughout the spring.

Slowly bring your awareness back to the present moment. Take a few deep breaths, feeling the energy of the meditation integrating into your being. When you are ready, open your eyes and embrace the new day, knowing that you have connected with the energy of Ostara and set your intentions for the season of rebirth and renewal.

Contents Needed for the Ritual:

Position the altar in the middle of the Circle, with its front facing the East Gate. Drape it with green, pink, or yellow cloths to reflect the sabbat colors. A floral arrangement of fresh-cut flowers on the altar is a spring tradition in many faiths. A package of seeds, a potted plant (preferably a white lily), and a basket of decorated eggs.

Consecrate the Area

[Add a pinch of salt to the bowl of water and hold it
toward the sky, asking this or similar blessings:]

I call upon the Blessed Trinity to
Consecrate this water and this salt for the
Elemental Purification of this Circle.
Representing my Goddess:
Of the Earth and Water of the Sea
So as I will it, So mote it be!

[Using the flame of a candle, light the incense,
and hold it toward the sky,
asking this or similar blessings:]

I call upon the Blessed Trinity to
Consecrate this flame and
This incense for the
Elemental Purification of this Circle.
Representing my God:
By Fire and Air, Glory to Thee
So as I will it, So mote It Be!

Elemental Chant

[Chant as you consecrate the Circle:]

Earth, my body;
Water my blood.
Air my breath; and
Fire my spirit.

Cast the Circle

I conjure Thee O Sacred Circle of Power
In this Perfect Place and This Perfect Hour
By Will and Grace encircling this Space
This joyous day I celebrate Ostara

For Health, Wealth, and Prosperity
As above, So below!
So as I will it, So mote it Be!

Call the Quarters

Hail to the stellar forces of nature
Keepers of the Watchtowers of the East
Wielders of Wind
I summon thee into this Circle
This Kyriat of Pilgrimage:
I invoke thee!
Welcome!

Hail to the stellar forces of nature
Keepers of the Watchtowers of the South
Wielders of Fire
I summon thee into this Circle
This Kyriat of Pilgrimage:
I invoke thee!
Welcome!

Hail to the stellar forces of nature
Keepers of the Watchtowers of the West
Wielders of Water
I summon thee into this Circle
This Kyriat of Pilgrimage:
I invoke thee!
Welcome!

Hail to the stellar forces of nature
Keeper of the Watchtowers of the North
Wielders of Earth
I summon thee into this Circle
This Kyriat of Pilgrimage:
I invoke thee!
Welcome!

Invocation of the Elohim

Hail to the Glorious Lord and Lady
Guardians of the Celestial Realm
Rulers of the Sun and Moon
Descend from the heavens and
Be with me to experience the
Magick and the Mysteries
Of this Rite of Ostara

The Kyriat of the Pilgrimage begins,
Leaving all that is familiar for
The trek for Enlightenment
The time has come when both light and darkness
Are of equal balance across the valleys.

The Yin and Yang energies
Of the God and Goddess present themselves
As the Sun and Moon
And the tango they dance
Fertilizes the fields with stability
Where young roots can take to fresh dirt
And spring forth in multitudes

Hosts of the Almighty Elohim
Welcome!

The Blessings of Ostara

On the first day of Spring, nature awakes,
We celebrate Ostara and the Earth's embrace.
The ground begins to thaw, the buds start to bloom,
And we embrace the blessings of this sacred season.

Ostara is a festival of balance and renewal,
Honoring the Equinox, the day and night are dual.
The sun's warmth returns, and we are transformed,
As life emerges, Nature is reborn.

Ostara, a time to honor the Lord and Lady of Spring,
Their energy stirs within us,
We plant the seeds of our dreams.
We feel Their presence with each gentle breeze,
Whispering secrets of growth and inner peace.

In this sacred space, we find harmony and connection
With Mother Earth, the Divine reflection.
With gratitude and love,
We honor the Earth's embrace, and
Celebrate Ostara with joy and grace.

The Goddess Speaks

Merry Meet Travel,
Spring Equinox has arrived
The world reawakens and
Blooms burst through
With new life and strength renewed.

As day and night are in perfect balance
The sprouts brought forth
From winter's frost are now
Beckoning the land for vitality

Gracing her face
Piercing her roots
As she thrives in the peak of exhilaration,
That occurs the fresh earth fields
Restored from the awakened
King of Light

Dear Traveler
And blossom my budding flower
Of wisdom and rejuvenation
As the sun rises in the east
And begins setting later in the west

When the hour of spark is evident
And life courses through the veins
Of all plants and animals alike
That has slumbered long and hard
And request the presence of his
Majesty To beam down radiance on the foliage
And quench the thirst of those once scorched
By freezing death
With rains of longevity and sustenance
Speak with me about your qualms with the dark
And let me pierce the bubble of the abyss
That shrouds you in tempests of blustery cold
So your heart may feel the warmth
Of love and growth

Bulbs sprout
And eggs hatch
Bringing with them from cherished respite
Both compassion and stamina
As nurturing hands mold them
Into beings of creation
And I, Mother Earth, bless them
To thrive and breathe
To rise and dazzle
The plains with color
As the vibrations of procreation
Steep my roots in everlasting
Love and harmony

Mysteries of the Cosmic Egg

As Above, So Below
As the Universe, So is the Soul
Within the Temple is the All-Seeing Eye
That sees beyond Heaven,
Earth and the Skies

The Serpent encircles
The Celestial Egg
The geometric act of manifestation
Waxes and wanes
As the Kundalini rises
The double helix unveils
The Inner Mysteries of the Ages
Craving Hermetic Knowledge
Ouroboros of the Sages

The Inner Mysteries of Creation
The Alpha and The Omega
Transforming the body
Allowing our Spirit to Transcend

Zoe, Maiden of Spring

The Wheel of the Year turns onward, and
The earth awakens,
As the days grow longer and winter fades,
The chill gives way to warmth:
Zoe, the Maiden of Spring
Glides gently upon the Earth, leaving a
Path of petals in Her wake.
With each breath, She exhales life,
Breathing vitality into the world around Her.

Zoe dances through meadows and swirls through the
Fields as Her joyful voice rings in the air.
She paints the landscape with vibrant colors as flowers
Bloom and trees burst with new leaves.

The world comes alive under Her tender touch,
As if awakening from a long and peaceful dream.
The sun begins to illuminate the sky,
Zoe speaks softly to the seeds
She cradles in Her youthful hands,
Encouraging them to come alive and

Flourish with each passing day.

She sees the potential for greatness in each tiny seed
Waiting to be nurtured and embraced,
As the rays of the Sun pour down from the sky,
Zoe rejoices in the return of light and warmth.

Just as Zoe breathes life into the world,
We, too, can breathe life into our
dreams and ambitions.
Allow the fresh liveliness of Springtime
To empower us, embracing the energy of
Renewal and growth.

May we dance with joy, like Zoe, and
Embrace the wonders of Nature
With vitality, comfort, and hope.

As we celebrate Ostara,
May the spirit of Zoe remind us
That life is a cycle, and
With each ending comes a new beginning.

Zoe, the Maiden of Spring,
Guide us on our journey of
Growth and transformation,
As we embrace the magic of
This season of renewal.

Ritual Observance

[Hold the seeds in your hand and say:]
Blessed are the seeds
Tossed to the ground
Sewing for the future
Sustenance the year around.

[Hold the Lily in your hand and say:]
Blessed is the Lily

A symbol of Death
The Beauty of the Goddess and
Peace with its whispering breath

[Hold the Egg in your hand and say:]
Blessed are the eggs
Colored beautiful and bright
Symbol of fertility
And the symbol of life

The Kyriat of Pilgrimage

On this day, I begin the Great Journey of
Self-discovery as I gather the tools to
Achieve stellar gnosis.
The Kyriat of the Pilgrimage
Is a spiritual trek that has been
Taken for thousands of years
By seekers around the world.
They did not know where this journey would
Lead them, nor do I, but
I will be brave:
I will not live in fear of the Unknown

The heights of Enlightenment
Are limitless, and
Awareness is the key.
I will continue to excel
The limitations of the flesh.
I believe the oral Teachings of the Mysteries
Lie hidden with me,
Reoccurring in every age.

I begin my pilgrimage of the Mysteries
That cannot be written on papyrus
Nor chiseled in clay. This knowledge
Lies not in libraries

In ancient books or tomes.
Perhaps it is stored in the
Akashic Records and calls to you
In the whisper of Spring rains.

Blessed Be the Trinity

Blessed be, my God:
Kyrie Eleison!
Blessed be, my Goddess:
Kyrie Eleison!
Blessed be, my Solar Lord:
Kyrie Eleison!

Blessings to our God
King of the heavens and cosmos
Father of sustenance and power
Our God of infinite existence

Blessings to our Goddess
Queen of the earth and seas
Mother of creation and fortitude
Our Goddess of infinite existence

Blessings to our Solar Son
Prince of peace and love
Son of sacrifice and selflessness
Our Solar Lord of infinite existence

Blessed Be the Trinity
Empower me on my Pilgrimage!
Kyrie Eleison, Kyrie Eleison
Kyrie Eleison!

Raising & Releasing Energy

As above, so below

Between my hands
I feel the energy grow!

To shape, mold, and create
That which only I can facilitate
The Circle within and
The Circle without
Neverending energy capable of
Magick and Miracles
From which all things
May be obtained:
So as I will it, So mote it be!

I now release this Energy of Ostara!

The Great Rite

As the Spear to the Cauldron,
The Lance to the Grail
Spirit to Flesh,
The Cakes and the Ale

The Alchemical Wedding
Unites the Lady and Lord;
Love makes One from Two
The Chalice and the Sword.

Feast and Libations

[Hold up the plate of cakes toward the heavens and say]
On this magickal day of Ostara, I celebrate
And share these cakes, symbolic of the
Grains that sustain my body:
I partake so that I may never hunger.

[Put a portion of the food on a separate plate
as a sign of thanks and communion.]

171

[Raise a chalice of wine or juice towards the heavens and say:]
On this magickal day of Ostara, I celebrate
And share this drink of the vine,
Symbolic of the blood of life:
I partake so that I may never thirst.
Blessed Be!

[Pour a portion of the wine onto the ground.]

Journal Your Thoughts

Thank the Deities

As this ritual of Ostara draws to a close,
I honor the Elohian Pantheon:
The wondrous Goddess, mighty God, and
Solar Lord Jesus.
Thank you for witnessing this Solar Rite
As you continue to bestow your essence of
Love and renewal each day.
Blessed Be the Trinity!

Dismiss the Quarters

I wish to thank the Stellar Forces of Nature
Keepers of the Watchtowers of the North
Those who wield Mother Earth
For being with me
This Kyriat of Pilgrimage:
Stay if you will; go if you must
Hail and Farewell!

I wish to thank the Stellar Forces of Nature
Keepers of the Watchtowers of the West
Those who wield Water and Intuition
For being with me
This Kyriat of Pilgrimage:

Stay if you will; go if you must
Hail and Farewell!

I wish to thank the Stellar Forces of Nature
Keepers of the Watchtowers of the South
Those who wield Fire and Flame
For being with me
This Kyriat of Pilgrimage:
Stay if you will; go if you must
Hail and Farewell!

I wish to thank the Stellar Forces of Nature
Keepers of the Watchtowers of the East
Those who wield Air and Wind
For being with me
This Kyriat of Pilgrimage:
Stay if you will; go if you must
Hail and Farewell!

Dismiss the Circle

This Rite of Ostara has now ended
The Wheel of the Year turns onward
The youthful Lord and Lady
Are in perfect balance
On this first day of Spring.

This Circle is open but never broken
May the peace of the Trinity
Be ever in your heart.
Merry we meet, and merry we part
'Til merry we meet again!
Blessed Be!

Beltane
May 1

Ritual Correspondences

Altar cloth: green
Candles: white, green, and yellow
Herbs: mint, rosemary, rue, blessed thistle
Stones: emerald, jade, peridot, opal, clear quartz
Observances: weaving flowered necklaces, head crowns, and chaplets.
Decorations: Maypole
Sabbat mythos: The Sacred Marriage of the God and Goddess
Sun position: Sun at 15 degrees Taurus
Tarot Card: The Lovers
Rune: Ehwaz
Angel: Chamuel

Beltane is the last of the fertility festivals, marking a midway point between spring and summer. It honors the Solar Lord and Earth Goddess in full bloom. On this day, the Solar Lord has flourished into a young man of vitality and strength and requests the hand of the Earth Goddess. Everywhere around us is a feeling of romance in the air, and underneath our feet lies a deep sensuality of life.

As part of Beltane's festivities, maypoles are erected to symbolize the Sacred Union between Lord and Lady on this rite. Maypoles have flowing ribbons that dancers hold to entwine each other while weaving in time to music, bringing these two energies together. The colors red and white represent the Divine Masculine and Feminine. Today, alternate color interpretations are used in any combination desired.

With Beltane comes a celebration of abundance, growth, vitality, sexuality, fertility, creativity, and joy; it is an occasion to honor our internal dualities and embrace them.

The Solar Lord and Goddess bring life. Their passion and love create abundance and joy for all humanity, signifying their sacred union and energy exchange. This ritual supports our innate appreciation of the planet's energy and the free flow of energy from our bodies to generate a tantric power of passionate desire for life itself. As Summer approaches, their consummation heralds a time of plenty.

The veneration of the Divine couple recognizes that both masculine and feminine energies are essential for creation. Both polarities must unite in harmony to manifest great things while internalizing that dynamic within us. We can use this ritual as guidance to embody those two energies and recognize how we can contribute meaningful work while maintaining a balance between our inner masculine and feminine aspects. In doing so, we will find ourselves continually energized and inspired by the love emanating from the Solar Lord and Goddess.

We can also use this ritual to honor special people who have shared their love and energy with us. By recognizing what our partners bring into our lives and celebrating them, we can be reminded of the importance of relationships and the power of love.

Consecrate the Area

[Add a pinch of salt to the bowl of water and hold it toward the sky, asking this or similar blessings:]

I call upon the Blessed Trinity to
Consecrate this water and this salt for the
Elemental Purification of this Circle.
Representing my Goddess:

Of the Earth and Water of the Sea
So as I will it, So mote it be!

[Using the flame of a candle, light the incense,
and hold it toward the sky,
asking this or similar blessings:]

I call upon the Blessed Trinity to
Consecrate this flame and
This incense for the
Elemental Purification of this Circle.
Representing my God:
By Fire and Air, Glory to Thee
So as I will it, So mote It Be!

Elemental Chant

[Chant as you consecrate the Circle:]

Earth, my body;
Water my blood.
Air my breath; and
Fire my spirit.

Cast the Circle

I summon and stir thee
Ancient Powers Within
Ancient Powers without -
O Sacred Temple
Surround me with your magnificence,
Encircle me with thy brilliance
Let the Energies Swirl and Build!
So as I will it, So mote it Be!

Call the Quarters

I call upon the Kingdom of Malkuth
Keepers of the Watchtowers of the East!
Roots of the Tree of Life
Elements of Air and Creativity
I summon and stir thee!
Attend this Circle and empower me
This day, I celebrate Beltane
I invoke thee:
Welcome!

I call upon the Kingdom of Malkuth
Keepers of the Watchtowers of the South!
Roots of the Tree of Life
Elements of Fire and Passion
I summon and stir thee!
Attend this Circle and empower me
This day, I celebrate Beltane
I invoke thee:
Welcome!

I call upon the Kingdom of Malkuth
Keepers of the Watchtowers of the West!
Roots of the Tree of Life
Elements of Water and Intuition
I summon and stir thee!
Attend this Circle and empower me
This day, I celebrate Beltane
I invoke thee:
Welcome!

I call upon the Kingdom of Malkuth
Keepers of the Watchtowers of the North!
Roots of the Tree of Life
Elements of Earth and Solidarity
I summon and stir thee!
Attend this Circle and empower me

This day, I celebrate Beltane
I invoke thee:
Welcome!

Invocation of the Blessed Trinity

Blessed Be this day of Beltane
Celebrating the Sacred Marriage of
Our God and Goddess
I invoke the Blessed Trinity:

Sacred Mother, Queen of the Earth and Seas
Mother of creation and life
Our Goddess of infinite existence

Divine Father, King of the Heavens and Cosmos
Father of sustenance and power
Our God of endless presence

Solar Lord, Prince of Peace and Charity
Son of sacrifice and selfless love
Our Great Teacher of Radiant Immortality:
Be with me to experience the
Magick and the Mysteries
In this Rite of Beltane,
I Invoke Thee:
Welcome!

The Blessings of Beltane

In the fullness of spring, when the earth is alive,
We gather to celebrate Beltane as the balefires thrive.
The days grow longer, the sun's warmth reigns,
And we embrace the blessings of this sacred flame.

Beltane is a festival of love and fertility,
We honor the Sacred Union of Divine Love's duality.

In this season of desire, we ignite the flame within,
Embracing our sensuality, shedding societal din.
We dance around the maypole, weaving ribbons bright,
In celebration of life's passions and delight.

Beltane, we honor the Lord and Lady in love,
Their energy ignites us like the Sun above.
We release inhibitions, opening to love's sweet call,
Embracing our true selves, unapologetically raw.

Beltane is a time of jubilation and passion so wild,
We gather in Circles and dance beguiled.
May the energy of this season set our souls ablaze,
Igniting our delights in this sacred space.

The Goddess Speaks

Merry Meet Traveler,
The Lord and I welcome you this day to
Witness this ritual of Sacred Union.
Celebrate with us our love and devotion.

We were like gravity and electricity,
Two powerful forces drawn together
Across infinite space.
When we collided, every molecule
Inside us shattered, erupting
Into a million pieces of stardust
that sparked a celestial explosion.

We embraced in an all-consuming
Force of cosmic power, shattering
The darkness of the primordial abyss
To create a brilliant new universe of light.

We merged our two existences together
to form something greater than ourselves and
as we did, the magickal energy

of our combined souls gave birth to you,
an image of both of us alive in this new world.

We bequeathed humanity our blessings:
A manifestation of heart and mind.
As you toil the land of the earth,
sowing your seed for nourishment
and life-giving abundance,
paving a path of grandeur and fertility.
Two souls merge together
in perfect sync and union,
Uniting through sublime grace and divinity.

Blessings of Beltane, Dear Traveler
May the Grace of this Solar Rite
Be a part of your
Ongoing Journey in this World and
In the Next:
Blessed Be!

The Wedding at Cana

Our Father who reigns in the Heavens
Comes to court His Beloved, Mother Earth
At the time of the season of Divine Love.
Gaia looks up to her Beloved
With great concern,
Saying:
"The grapes are young on the vine,
These fruits need your Sacred Waters
Or else there will be no Wine
For the Wedding Feast!"

Her Consort kindly replies,
"Youthful Lady of the Gardens,
Glorious Mother of
The figs, olives, and wheat,
Worry not!

I will send our Sun to draw water
From the lakes and rivers into
My fertile clouds.
In joy and fulfillment, I will release
The waters of the firmament
Onto Your abundant earth."

Her Consort proudly declares,
"I promise this vow to
All in attendance,
The House of Bread shall
Prosper and the Feast
Will be complete.
On this Day of Sacred Marriage
The Bride and Groom will have Wine."

The Wedding Vows

[Vows of the Maiden]
My Beloved is white and ruddy,
The chiefest among ten thousand.
His head is of the finest gold.
His locks are bushy and black as a raven:
His eyes are the eyes of doves

By the rivers of water,
Washed with milk, moreover, fitly set.
His cheeks are as a bed of spices,
As sweet flowers:
His lips were like lilies,
Dropping sweet-smelling myrrh:
His hands are as gold rings with beryl;
His belly is as bright as ivory
Overlaid with Sapphires

His legs are like pillars of marble,
Set upon sockets of fine gold:
His countenance is as excellent
As the cedars
His mouth is altogether lovely:
This is my Beloved, and this is my Friend.

[Vows of the Bridegroom]
How beautiful are thy feet with sandals!
The joints of thy thighs are like jewels
The work of the hands of a craftsman
Thy navel is like a round goblet
Which wanteth not liquor
Thy Belly is like wheat set about with lilies.
Thy two breasts are like two young roes
That are twins.

Thy Neck is a Tower of Ivory
Thine Eyes are like glistening Pools
How fair and how pleasant art thou,
O love, for delights!
Thy stature is like a palm tree,
And thy breast clusters of grapes.

In my thoughts,
I will go up to the palm tree,
And I will take hold of the boughs thereof:
And thy breasts shall be as Clusters of the Vine,
And the smell of thy nose like apples;

And the roof of thy mouth
Like the best wine for my Beloved,
That goeth down sweetly,
Causing the lips of those that
Are asleep to Speak.

[Reply Vows of the Maiden]
I am My Beloved's, and his desire is toward me.
Come now, My Beloved
Let us go forth into the field
Let us lodge in the villages
Let us get up early
To the vineyards
Let us see if the vine flourished
Whether the tender grape appears,
And the pomegranates bud forth:
There will I give thee my loves.

The mandrakes give a smell,
And at our gates are all manner
Of pleasant fruits,
New and old,
Which I have laid up for you,
O My Beloved.

The Crowning of the May Queen/King

[Places the Ring of Flowers on your head:]
My Beloved Bride/Groom
I place this Ring of Flowers
Upon my head
Symbolic of unity and love
Twin flames, Twin souls
Forever joined and intertwined
Together, dancing the Maypole
I promise never to leave your side
As you have never left mine.

The Essence of Youth and Vibrancy
My Beloved Bride/Bridegroom
Handsome Lover/Fair Maiden of Spring
With this Ring of Flowers
I Crown the May Queen/King!

[Take the first and third candles and light the center candle.]

Raising & Releasing Energy

As above, So below
Between my hands
I feel the energy grow!

To shape, mold, and create
That which only I can facilitate
The Circle within and
The Circle without
Neverending energy capable of
Magick and Miracles
From which all things
May be obtained:
So as I will it, So mote it be!

I now release this Energy of Beltane!

The Great Rite

As the Spear to the Cauldron,
The Lance to the Grail
Spirit to Flesh,
The Cakes and the Ale

The Alchemical Wedding
Unites the Lady and Lord;
Love makes One from Two
The Chalice and the Sword.

Feast and Libations

[Hold up the plate of cakes toward the heavens and say:]
On this powerful day of Beltane, I celebrate
And share these cakes, symbolic of the
Grains that sustain my body:
I partake so that I may never hunger.

[Put a portion of the food on a separate plate
as a sign of thanks and communion.]

[Raise a chalice of wine or juice towards the heavens and say:]
On this powerful day of Beltane, I celebrate
and share this drink of the vine,
Symbolic of the blood of life:
I partake so that I may never thirst.
Blessed Be!

[Pour a portion of the wine onto the ground.]

Journal Your Thoughts

Thank the Deities

As this ritual of Beltane draws to a close,
I Honor the Elohian Pantheon:
My wondrous Goddess, mighty God, and
Solar Lord Jesus.
Thank you for witnessing this Solar Rite
You continue to bestow your essence of
Life, love, and renewal each day.
Blessed Be the Trinity!

Dismiss the Quarters

Kingdom of Malkuth
Watchtowers of the North:

I thank you for your presence
As I celebrate the Celestial Union of Beltane
Stay if you will; go if you must
Hail and Farewell!

Kingdom of Malkuth
Watchtowers of the West:
I thank you for your presence
As I celebrate the Celestial Union Of Beltane
Stay if you will; go if you must
Hail and Farewell!

Kingdom of Malkuth
Watchtowers of the South:
I thank you for your presence
As I celebrate the Celestial Union of Beltane
Stay if you will; go if you must
Hail and Farewell!

Kingdom of Malkuth
Watchtowers of the East:
I thank you for your presence
As I celebrate the Celestial Union of Beltane
Stay if you will; go if you must
Hail and Farewell!

Dismiss the Circle

This Rite of Beltane has now ended
The Wheel of the Year turns onward
I have witnessed the Sacred Marriage of
The Solar King and the Lunar Queen
As abundant energy abounds!

This Circle is open but never broken.
May the peace of the Trinity
Be ever in your heart.
Merry we meet, and merry we part,

'til merry, we meet again!
Blessed Be!

Midsummer: The Kyriat of Initiation
June 21

Ritual Correspondences

Altar cloth: red or bright yellow
Candles: white, red, and gold
Herbs: honeysuckle, lavender, mint, roses, feverfew
Stones: amber, jet, cat's eye, bloodstone, garnet, ruby
Observances: Foot washing and rededication to the Trinity, the sun
Is at its zenith, spell casting encouraged
Decorations: summer flowers, sun wheels
Sabbat Mythos: The Goddess is a Mother, pregnant with Her Consort's
Promised Child.
Sun position: Sun is 0 degrees Cancer
Tarot Card: The Star
Rune: Kenaz
Angel: Michael

Summer Solstice is the longest day of the year, with the shortest night. Despite its name, Midsummer marks the first day of summer. The Wheel of the Year comes to a half-circle. The growing season is in full bloom as farmers tend to their summer crops. The Solar Lord and Goddess extend their blessings of fertility across the land.

Today, the Solar Lord is honored at his peak of power. After today, our God will begin to age, and the romance of Beltane has strengthened the bond between the two lovers. The Solar God smiles down on the fields with his blessing of growth and plentifulness.

This Goddess stands by his side with a smile as they revel in the Light of creation that shines down from the Solar God onto the fields of sustenance. From darkness comes the Light; from shadows of perpetual hardship, the Light blossomed over time into a shining ray of hope. The bonfires are lit in reflection of the Sun for this Fire festival. Through the lens of Trinitarian Wicca, Mid-Summer is equally a water festival, as the Goddess initiates Her children reborn from Her Cosmic womb in the waters of Initiation.

Noon Summer Solstice Meditation

Find a comfortable and quiet space. Close your eyes, and take a few deep breaths to center yourself. Embrace the sun's energy as it rises with the day. Visualize yourself in a vibrant summer landscape surrounded by the beauty of nature. Feel the sun's warmth on your skin and the season's energy.

As you breathe in, imagine that you are drawing in the energy of the sun, absorbing its vitality and strength. Feel the warmth and brightness filling your entire being. As you exhale, release any tension or worries, letting go of anything that no longer serves you. Allow the sun's energy to cleanse and rejuvenate your mind, body, and spirit—feeding all your cells, organs, chakras, and subtle bodies with vibrant energy and life force.

Take another deep breath and observe the sun's healing power as it ignites within you its unique essence. Allow this essence to move through you like a powerful wave of warmth and expansion. Allow that essence to fill your entire being, bringing vitality to every aspect of your existence.

As you continue to bask in this energy, consider any intentions or goals you wish for abundance in this season. Picture them becoming a reality in vivid detail - imagine how they will look, feel, smell, and taste when they manifest for you now. Feel these intentions become real as they join with the solar energy radiating from within you.

As you return to the moment, give thanks for the beauty of this experience, and all that life offers; for its abundance, vitality, joys, and possibilities; for its lessons taught and lessons still yet to learn; for its magic that never ceases to amaze us all! Give thanks for being alive at such an auspicious time in history–sending out love into our world! Take a few more moments before emerging from your meditation, feeling nourished on all levels from above!

Needed for the Ritual

Water is all that is necessary for the foot-washing portion of the ritual; however, you may add herbs, oils, and magickal waters of your choice. A suggestion is adding three shakes of Florida Water, ½ dram of vanilla, ½ dram of lemongrass fragrance oil, and less than a handful of each herb: roses, lavender, and chamomile. This mixture is fresh and invigorating yet calming and rejuvenating.

Consecrate the Area

[Add a pinch of salt to the bowl of water and hold it toward the sky, asking this or similar blessings:]

I call upon the Blessed Trinity to
Consecrate this water and this salt for the
Elemental Purification of this Circle.
Representing my Goddess:
Of the Earth and Water of the Sea —
So as I will it, So mote it be!

[Using the flame of a candle, light the incense, and hold it toward the sky, asking this or similar blessings:]

I call upon the Blessed Trinity to
Consecrate this flame and
This incense for the
Elemental Purification of this Circle.

Representing my God:
By Fire and Air, Glory to Thee
So as I will it, So mote It Be!

Elemental Chant

[Chant as you consecrate the Circle:]

Earth, my body;
Water my blood.
Air my breath; and
Fire my spirit.

Cast the Circle

I call upon the natural energies of
Mother Earth and the
Stellar Universal Powers!
I cast and summon the Circle of power
As I assemble the Sacred Temple:
This joyous day I celebrate Litha
As above, so below
So as I will it, So Mote it Be!

Call the Quarters

O Ancient Ones
Guardians of the Watchtowers of the East
Keepers of the element of Air
I summon and stir thee
Aid me in my Midsummer workings
On this Kyriat of Initiation
I invoke thee!
Welcome!

O Ancient Ones

Guardians of the Watchtowers of the South
Keepers of the element of Fire
I summon and stir thee
Aid me in my Midsummer workings
On this Kyriat of Initiation
I invoke thee!
Welcome!

O Ancient Ones
Guardians of the Watchtowers of the West
Keepers of the element of Water
I summon and stir thee
Aid me in my Midsummer workings
On this Kyriat of Initiation
I invoke thee!
Welcome!

O Ancient Ones
Guardians of the Watchtowers of the North
Keepers of the element of Earth
I summon and stir thee
Aid me in my Midsummer workings
On this Kyriat of Initiation
I invoke thee!
Welcome!

Invocation of the Elohim

Hail to the Glorious Lord and Lady
Guardians of the Celestial Realm
Rulers of the Sun and Moon
Sovereign engineers of the Constellations
Descend from the heavens and assemble here
Be with me to experience the
Magick and the Mysteries
Of this Midsummer Rite

The Kyriat of Initiation

Acknowledges the seekers of
Ancient Wisdom and
Hidden Knowledge symbolized by
The sacred waters through
Anointing, Washing,
Cleansing and Submersion.

Water from Water,
As below, so above
Seek the Ancient secrets
And be mystically reborn
From the Womb of the Dove

Hosts of the Almighty Elohim
Welcome!

The Blessings of Summer Solstice

Daylight lingers with a celestial dance,
The Sun's radiant grace
Fills the world with warmth as nature meets.
The longest day, a gift of golden hours,
An offering of time to soak in life's embrace,
Blossoms unfurl in vibrant hues:
A symphony of colors adorned with grace.

The sun, a blazing orb, its brilliance unfurled,
Casting its glow upon fields and streams,
Reviving spirits, igniting dreams.

Summer Solstice is a sacred pause,
An invitation to revel in nature's bounty,
To embrace the sun's caress on skin and soul,
And feel the pulse of life in every ounce of me.

The air is alive with whispers of
Happiness and mirth,
A chorus of laughter beneath the blue sky,

As we bask in the warmth of nature's embrace,
Grateful blessings that summer brings nigh.

Summer Solstice, your gifts are boundless,
A reminder of the cycles that govern all,
A time to reflect, to celebrate, to cherish,
The blessings of life, both big and small.

So let us raise our voices in gratitude and praise,
For Litha, the sabbat so grand,
May its light guide us each passing day,
As we journey together, hand in hand.

The Goddess Speaks

The Solar Lord is at His zenith,
Burning hot and bright
With its brilliant rays of vitality
Shining longest on this day.

The Great Mother
takes His life-energy into
The blossoming grains, fruit,
Flowers and foliage of the earth.

Merry Meet Traveler,
My message to you is LIVE!
Seize the day! Work and play,
Live and love and
Be present in the moment:
The seeds you so thoughtfully sewed
In the Spring, have taken root and
Thrive in the Summer sun!

Blessings of Summer Solstice,
Dear Traveler
May the Grace of this Sabbat
Be a part of your

Ongoing Journey in this World and
In the Next:
Blessed Be!

The Kyriat of Initiation

Summer Solstice honors
The Kyriat of Initiation
The day of Enlightenment that
The Great Salvation is one
I must achieve by looking within;
As I open my eyes to the Unveiled Truth
I am now capable of sight for the first time
Once the clouds of dogma lift.

The heights of Enlightenment
Are limitless, and
Awareness is the key.
I will continue to excel
The limitations of the flesh.
The oral teachings of the Mysteries
Lie hidden within,
Reoccurring in every age.

I rededicate myself on this day
Through immersion in the Spirit,
Returning to the Great Womb:
The symbolic waters of baptism.

John the Baptist
The Dark King, both predecessor and initiator,
Immersed the souls in the spring waters
Of the Great Mother
The Creatrix of life and vessel of death
And as the water ran through his hands
The impurities melted into the water
Invoking humility and empathy
In his actions

And restored the righteous heart
Of humankind.

The Interceding of the Goddess

Elizabeth and Mary:
Filled with the Spirit of the Goddess;
Were the earthly Mothers of
John the Initiator and of
Jesus, the Solar Lord:

Twin Kings, One of Light and One of Dark
Meeting twice a year on
the longest day and the longest night
The King of Holly and the King of Oak
Strike their mighty swords of
Peace and Enlightenment.

The journey to self-discovery is the key
To unlock inner wisdom.
From the Initiator comes the spark of gnosis
Igniting the Solar Lord's
Power of the Sun!

Twice a year, the Dueling Kings reflect
The Circle of the Year
Rising and falling to rise again!

Blessed Be the Trinity

Blessed be the God
Kyrie Eleison!
Blessed be the Goddess
Kyrie Eleison!
Blessed be the Solar Lord
Kyrie Eleison!

Blessings to the God

King of the heavens and cosmos
Father of sustenance and power
Our God of infinite existence.

Blessings to the Goddess
Queen of the Earth and Seas
Mother of creation and fortitude
Our Goddess of infinite existence.

Blessings to the Solar Son
Prince of peace and love
Son of sacrifice and selflessness
Our Solar Lord of infinite existence.

Blessed Be the Trinity
This Kyriat of Initiation
Kyrie Eleison, Kyrie Eleison
Kyrie Eleison!

Foot Washing

Blessed are you, Great Goddess,
The source of Living Water,
Womb of creation and
The way of self-salvation
With humility and empathy.

Sacred water, herbs, and oil
Cleanses the body,
Awakens the mind and
Revives the soul.

Raising & Releasing Energy

As above, so below
Between my hands
I feel the energy grow!

To shape, mold, and create
That which only I can facilitate
The Circle Within and
The Circle Without
Neverending energy capable of
Magick and Miracles
From which all things
May be obtained:
So as I will it, So mote it be!

I now release this Energy of Litha!

The Great Rite

As the Spear to the Cauldron,
The Lance to the Grail
Spirit to Flesh,
The Cakes and the Ale

The Alchemical Wedding
Unites the Lady and Lord;
Love makes One from Two
The Chalice and the Sword.

Feast and Libations

[Hold up the plate of cakes toward the heavens and say:]
On this magickal day of Midsummer, I celebrate
And share these cakes, symbolic of the
Grains that sustain my body:
I partake so that I may never hunger.

[Put a portion of the food on a separate plate
as a sign of thanks and communion.]

[Raise a chalice of wine or juice towards the heavens and say:]
On this magickal day of Midsummer, I celebrate
and share this drink of the vine,

Symbolic of the blood of life:
I partake so that I may never thirst.
Blessed Be!

[Pour a portion of the wine onto the ground.]

Journal Your Thoughts

Thank the Deities

As this ritual of Midsummer draws to a close,
I honor the Elohian pantheon:
My wondrous Goddess, mighty God, and
Solar Lord Jesus.
Thank you for witnessing this Solar Rite
As You continue to bestow your essence of
Life, love, and renewal each day.
Blessed Be the Trinity!

Dismiss the Quarters

I wish to thank the Ancient Ones
Guardians of the Watchtowers of the North
Keepers of Mother Earth
For being with me to celebrate
The Kyriat of Initiation
Stay if you Will - Go if you Must
Hail and Farewell!

I wish to thank the Ancient Ones
Guardians of the Watchtowers of the West
Keepers of Water and Intuition
For being with me to celebrate
The Kyriat of Initiation
Stay if you Will - Go if you Must
Hail and Farewell!

I wish to thank the Ancient Ones
Guardians of the Watchtowers of the South
Keepers of Fire and Flame
For being with me to celebrate
The Kyriat of Initiation
Stay if you Will - Go if you Must
Hail and Farewell!

I wish to thank the Ancient Ones
Guardians of the Watchtowers of the East
Keepers of the Air and Wind
For being with me to celebrate
The Kyriat of Initiation
Stay if you Will - Go if you Must
Hail and Farewell!

Dismiss the Circle

This Rite of Midsummer has now ended
The Wheel of the Year turns onward
I have entered the realm of initiation,
As my Goddess now carries the Promised Child
And my God reigns at His zenith of power.

This Circle is open but never broken
May the peace of the Trinity
Be ever in your heart.
Merry we meet, and merry we part
'Til merry we meet again!
Blessed Be!

Lammas
August 1

Ritual Correspondences

Altar cloth: gold or dark green
Candles: yellow, orange, dark green
Herbs: goldenrod, ivy, myrtle, sunflowers, mums
Stones: black tourmaline, tiger's eye, citrine, lodestones
Observances: Baking loaves of bread, making corn dollies and crowns,
Burning of the Judas Man, modern self-sacrifices to charity
Decorations: summer flowers, sun
Sabbat Mythos: The self-sacrifice of the Solar God infuses the Earth
for harvest, and the Goddess is heavy with His Child.
Sun position: Sun is 15 degrees Leo
Tarot Card: The Hanged Man
Rune: Ingwaz
Angel: Jophiel

Lammas, nestled between the Summer Solstice and Autumn Equinox, heralds the commencement of the bountiful harvest festivities. It is a joyous occasion where people unite, sharing delectable food, enchanting music, and spirited dance. The heart of this solar festival revolves around creating a special loaf of bread, known as the Lammas loaf, crafted from the first grains of the harvest. It is also a time for introspection and gratitude as individuals express their appreciation for the abundance in their lives and set intentions for the months ahead. The name Lammas finds its roots in the Anglo-Saxon term "half-masse" or Loaf Mass, as these loaves were lovingly baked with the initial grains and offered to the Church for blessings.

Lammas, also known as Lughnasadh, pays homage to the Celtic Sun God Lugh. However, since Lugh is not the Solar Lord in Trinitarian Wicca, Lammas is the more fitting choice for this tradition, as it acknowledges the spirit of Jesus. Including loaves of bread in the parable of feeding the 5,000, coupled with the symbolism of fish representing the Piscean Solar Lord, seamlessly aligns with the essence of Lammas.

Corn Dollie figures also hold significance during Lammas, symbolizing reverence and gratitude for the Solar Lord's sacrifice of His life force to nourish the earth. These figures are meticulously crafted from the green husks of corn and left to dry. Placing them on altars adds to the enchanting spirit of the season. Bundling sheaves of wheat tied at the center creates festive and symbolic door and bough decorations, representing the abundance and gratitude for the blessings bestowed upon us. Corn Dollie figures are straw work, an integral part of the handmade harvest customs of Europe. They are believed to embody the spirit of the corn, or grain, within the crop. To ensure a prosperous harvest the following year, the corn dollies are ceremoniously plowed into the first trough of the new season.

During Lammas, the Solar Lord selflessly sacrifices His life force, infusing it into the earth to fortify the growth cycles for the upcoming two harvests. It is crucial to comprehend that His passing is not immediate or a cruel punishment, but a precious bestowal of life-sustaining essence that provides additional nourishment for the harvest. The reaping of wheat sheaves and corn stalks symbolizes the act of self-sacrifice for the betterment of humanity, initiating the Solar Lord's final stages of His annual journey. The waning light and warmth of the sun mirror His diminishing vitality. From Lammas until Mabon, the Young Lord gracefully transforms into the Aging God, steadily declining until Samhain when He descends into the Underworld, patiently awaiting rebirth at Yule. Thanks to the Sage's essence, gifted to us, the earth remains abundant, even during winter.

Consecrate the Area

[Add a pinch of salt to the bowl of water and hold it
toward the sky, asking this or similar blessings:]

I call upon the Blessed Trinity to
Consecrate this water and this salt for the
Elemental Purification of this Circle.
Representing my Goddess:
Of the Earth and Water of the Sea
So as I will it, So mote it be!

[Using the flame of a candle, light the incense,
and hold it toward the sky,
asking this or similar blessings:]

I call upon the Blessed Trinity to
Consecrate this flame and
This incense for the
Elemental Purification of this Circle.
Representing my God:
By Fire and Air, Glory to Thee
So as I will it, So mote It Be!

Elemental Chant

[Chant as you consecrate the Circle:]

Earth, my body;
Water my blood.
Air my breath; and
Fire my spirit.

Cast the Circle

I call and gather the Strength
Of the Holy Ancient Powers
To encircle me with your Energy
To lead me and guide me
This joyous day I celebrate Lammas
Arise! Arise! Arise!
So as I will it, So mote it Be!

Call the Quarters

Harken Unto Me
O Shining Ones of the East
Ancient Keepers of the Watchtowers
The Powers of Wind and Air
Bless me as I celebrate
The First Harvest of Lammas
I Invoke thee!
Welcome!

Harken Unto Me
O Shining Ones of the South
Ancient Keepers of the Watchtowers
The Powers of Fire and Flame
Bless me as I Celebrate
The First Harvest of Lammas
I Invoke thee!
Welcome!

Harken Unto Me
O Shining Ones of the West
Ancient Keepers of the Watchtowers
The Powers of Water and Intuition
Bless me as I Celebrate
The First Harvest of Lammas
I Invoke thee!
Welcome!

Harken Unto Me
O Shining Ones of the North
Ancient Keepers of the Watchtowers
The Powers of Mother Earth
Bless me as I Celebrate
The First Harvest of Lammas
I Invoke thee!
Welcome!

Invocation of the Blessed Trinity

Blessed Be this day of Lammas
Celebrating the First Harvest and
The sacrifice of the Solar Lord
I invoke the Blessed Trinity:

Sacred Mother, Queen of the Earth and Seas
Mother of creation and life
Our Goddess of infinite existence

Divine Father, King of the Heavens and Cosmos
Father of sustenance and power
Our God of endless presence

Solar Lord, Prince of Peace and Charity
Son of sacrifice and selfless love
Our Solar Lord of radiant immortality:

Be with me to experience the
Magick and the Mysteries
In this Rite of Lammas,
I Invoke Thee:
Welcome!

The Blessings of Lammas

In the embrace of the summer sun,
We are immersed in the blessings of Lammas.

As the days grow longer, and
The earth yields its First Harvest,
We gather to honor the surrounding abundance.

Lammas, the Festival of first fruits,
Calls us to give thanks for the gifts of the land.
It is a time of gratitude and appreciation
For the nourishment that sustains us,
Physically, mentally, and spiritually.

From the golden wheat to the vibrant fruits,
We are reminded of the cycle of life and
The generosity of nature.
Lammas is a time of celebration,
We break bread, sharing the fruits of our labor.

Like the grains of wheat that are threshed,
We shed the old and make way for the new.
Lammas reminds us of the continuous
Cycle of growth and transformation
Inherent in our lives and
The importance of gratitude and reciprocity.
Just as the earth provides for us,
We must also give back in equal measure.

In this season of harvest,
May the blessings of Lammas guide us
On our journey of growth and inspire us to
Nurture the seeds of abundance and generosity,
Sharing our gifts with others.

The Goddess Speaks

Merry Meet, Dear Traveler!
Join me on a stroll through the
Prosperous lands of plenty.
Today's festival of the
First Harvest brings abundance

209

In the fields, orchards, and
Gardens as the crops reach their peak!

When the sheaths of wheat and
The stalks of corn are struck,
The sickle brings the annual
Celestial sacrifice of the Solar Lord
To sustain the Earth through
The coming winter.

My Beloved Consort will spill
His Divine Lifeforce and
I will absorb it for the enrichment
Of our beautiful planet
Until his rebirth at Yule.

The Grains will make loaves of bread
And the Grapes will make wines,
The fruits and vegetables will be
Preserved so that Humanity
Will not hunger, nor thirst.

His brilliant solar rays will continue
To diminish light and heat
As the Wheel of the Year turns on.
His sacrifice establishes no martyr
And His gift demands no settlement:
Instead, celebrate His selflessly given love
With joyful gratefulness.

Blessings of this sacred time,
Dear Traveler,
May the grace of Lammas
Accompany you on your ongoing journey
In this world and the next:
Blessed Be!

Crowning of the Corn King

Without sacrifice, nothing is gained
The wheat, barley, corn, and oat grains
Separating the wheat from the shaft, and
They keep from the rows;
Into the fire, the Judas Man goes!
[Toss the corn shuck dolly into the fire]

I crown my head with a wreath of green
Honoring the sacrifice of the Corn King.
[Place a wreath of green shucks on your head.]

Ode to the Dying and Rising Deities

The tale of Corn King,
Sympathetic and wise
Self-sacrificing
For all the world.
On this day, I honor
The Sacrificial Solar Lords
Throughout all time
The godman in each of us.

The Dying and the Risen
You are God, you are human,
You are part of Nature and the Earth
You are the yellow brilliance
Bright as the Sun.
To enrich us, to sustain us
All year long.

Raising & Releasing Energy

As above, so below
Between my hands
I feel the energy grow!

To shape, mold, and create
That which only I can facilitate
The Circle Within and
The Circle Without
Neverending energy capable of
Magick and Miracles
From which all things
May be obtained:
So as I will it, So mote it be!

I now release this Energy of Lammas!

The Great Rite

As the Spear to the Cauldron,
The Lance to the Grail
Spirit to Flesh,
The Cakes and the Ale

The Alchemical Wedding
Unites the Lady and Lord;
Love makes One from Two
The Chalice and the Sword.

Feast and Libations

[Hold up the plate of cakes toward the heavens and say:]
On this magickal day of Lammas, I celebrate
And share these cakes, symbolic of the
Grains that sustain my body:
I partake so that I may never hunger.

[Put a portion of the food on a separate plate
as a sign of thanks and communion.]

[Raise a chalice of wine or juice towards the heavens and say:]
On this magickal day of Lammas, I celebrate
and share this drink of the vine,

Symbolic of the blood of life:
I partake so that I may never thirst.
Blessed Be!

[Pour a portion of the wine onto the ground.]

Journal Your Thoughts

Thank the Deities

As this ritual of Lammas draws to a close,
I Honor the Elohian Pantheon:
My wondrous Goddess, mighty God, and
Solar Lord Jesus.
Thank you for witnessing this Solar Rite
As You continue to bestow your essence of
Life, love, and renewal each day.
Blessed Be the Trinity!

Dismiss the Quarters

I wish to thank the Shining Ones of the North
Ancient Keepers of the Watchtowers
The Powers of Mother Earth For being with me
This Rite of Lammas
Stay if you will; go if you must
Hail and Farewell!

I wish to thank the Shining Ones of the West
Ancient Keepers of the Watchtowers
Powers of the Waters and Oceans
For being with me
This Rite of Lammas
Stay if you will; go if you must
Hail and Farewell!

I wish to thank the Shining Ones of the South

Ancient Keepers of the Watchtowers
Powers of Fire and Flame
For being with me
This Rite of Lammas
Stay if you will; go if you must
Hail and Farewell!

I wish to thank the Shining Ones of the East
Ancient Keepers of the Watchtowers
Powers of the Air and Winds
For being with me
This Rite of Lammas
Stay if you will; go if you must
Hail and Farewell!

Dismiss the Circle

This rite of Lammas has now ended,
The Wheel of the Year turns onward,
The first harvest has been honored
The Solar Lord has offered his last ounce of energy
unto the Earth
The reaping now begins for the
Seeds sown.

This Circle is open but never broken.
May the peace of the Trinity
Be ever in your heart.
Merry we meet, and merry we part,
'til merry, we meet again!
Blessed Be!

Mabon: Kyriat of the Feast
September 21

Ritual Correspondences

Altar cloth: orange, gold, or brown
Candles: maroon, orange, gold
Herbs: marigolds, sunflowers, hibiscus, myrrh
Stones: amber, jet, tiger's eye, peridot, yellow topaz
Observances: celebratory feast
Decorations: grapes, vine garlands, Indian corn, cornucopia
Sabbat Mythos: Goddess becomes a Crone as God's essence
enriches the bountiful feast.
Tarot: The Hermit
Sun position: Sun is at 0 degrees Libra
Tarot Card: The Hermit
Rune: Gebo
Angel: Metatron

Mabon, or the Autumn Equinox, is the second harvest festival and the midpoint between the summer and winter solstices. Farmers prepare their fields to lie fallow in the winter months, and wine is made from the ripened grapes of summer. The Autumn Equinox is a time of balance between light and dark and the recognition of the transformation of the seasons and the cyclic nature of life.

Mabon originates in agricultural societies, particularly those that depended on the land for survival. Our Aging God continues His decline after surrendering His life force at Lammas to sustain the crops until the harvest season ends at Samhain. This is a time to express gratitude and to reflect on the previous year.

Our Goddess is now a Crone, and our God is the Dying Solar Lord who will feast his last night with friends and family. Trinitarian Wiccans recognize the Archangel Michael as the celestial intermediary that takes on the role of spiritual warrior in the absence of the Aging God until the Solar Lord is reborn at Yule. Michael represents courage, protection, and guidance, and by celebrating Michaelmas, participants can find inspiration to overcome adversity.

Evening Mabon Meditation

This Mabon meditation is designed to help you connect with the energy of Mabon and embrace the balance of light and dark. It is a time of balance and gratitude as we transition from the abundance of summer to the introspection of fall. Twilight, the magical time between day and night, is perfect for a Mabon meditation.

Find a comfortable, quiet place to sit or lie down. Close your eyes and focus on your breath. Breathe in deeply through your nose, feeling the air fill your lungs, then gently exhale through your mouth and feel yourself begin to relax deeper with each breath.

When you are ready, close your eyes and imagine yourself in a tranquil autumn landscape full of the wonders of nature. As you inhale, absorb the vibes of harmony and balance that fill the air. While you exhale, release any stress and tension that no longer serves you. Focus on being present as the sun sets. Now, shift your focus to your heart center, visualizing a brilliant golden light emanating from it. This is a sign of gratitude and abundance.

Notice a circle drawn in the earth around you of corn husks, dried herbs, pinecones, and acorns: symbols of autumn abundance and harvest time. Stand within this circle feeling connected to nature's rhythms and cycles as they surround you.

Now reflect upon both sides of this Equinox, the lightness of summer's end and the darkness that comes with autumn's arrival. Feel both energies merging in perfect balance inside you until there is no separation between them, only harmony. Allow these energies to fill you until they overflow from within you into every aspect of your life.

When ready, open your eyes slowly and take a few moments to ground yourself before returning to reality—taking this feeling of balance with you!

Consecrate the Area

[Add a pinch of salt to the bowl of water and hold it toward the sky, asking this or similar blessings:]

I call upon the Blessed Trinity to
Consecrate this water and this salt for the
Elemental Purification of this Circle.
Representing my Goddess:
Of the Earth and Water of the Sea
So as I will it, So mote it be!"

[Using the flame of a candle, light the incense,
and hold it toward the sky,
asking this or similar blessings:]

I call upon the Blessed Trinity to
Consecrate this flame and
This incense for the
Elemental Purification of this Circle.
Representing my God:
By Fire and Air, Glory to Thee
So as I will it, So mote It Be!

Elemental Chant

[Chant as you consecrate the Circle:]

Earth, my body;
Water my blood.
Air my breath; and
Fire my spirit.

Cast the Circle

I cast this Circle around me times three
The energy flows below me
As the heavens tower above me
Balancing the Sun and Moon on
This magickal day of Mabon
So as I will it, So mote it be!

Call the Quarters

Hail to the Elements, Divine
The building blocks of our existence
Keepers of the Watchtowers of the East
The Powers of Wind and Air
Be with me this Kyriat of the Feast
I Invoke thee!
Welcome!

Hail to the Elements, Divine
The building blocks of our existence
Keepers of the Watchtowers of the South
The Powers of Fire and Flame
Be with me this Kyriat of the Feast
I Invoke thee!
Welcome!

Hail to the Elements, Divine
The building blocks of our existence

Keepers of the Watchtowers of the West
The Power of Water and Intuition
Be with me this Kyriat of the Feast
I Invoke thee!
Welcome!

Hail to the Elements, Divine
The building blocks of our existence
Keepers of the Watchtowers of the North
The Powers of Mother Earth
Be with me this Kyriat of the Feast
I Invoke thee!
Welcome!

Invocation of the Elohim

Hail to the Glorious Lord and Lady
The Eternal Council of El:
Known by their many names!
Guardians of the Celestial Realm
Rulers of the Sun and Moon
Sovereign engineers of the Constellations
Descend from the Heavens and assemble here
Be with me to experience the
Magick and the Mysteries
Of this rite of Mabon

The Kyriat of the Feast
Salutes the sacrifice of the
Aging God who provides the
Living world with
Nourishment and sustenance.

Bread of Life,
Fruit of the Vine
The fruits and grains of sacrifice
Reaped from the sown fields
Imbued with the essence of the Divine

To sustain and keep my Soul plenty
Through the coming darkness of
Winter's repose.

Hosts of the Almighty Elohim
Welcome!

The Goddess Speaks

Merry Meet Traveler
On this day when dark and light
Are in perfect balance,
So are our emotions.
We give thanks for our bountiful harvest
Which will provide for the world
Until spring.
So we will celebrate a great feast with
His friends and family.
We will laugh over good times of
Passing year....

This Great Feast of Mabon
We honor His selfless gift.
Our Aging Solar Lord
Freely sacrificed His own life
So that the world may live, eat, and
Be healthy and thrive.
He will shed His own blood to
Enrich the waning earth
Giving life to all who partake.
Here, I will remain in solitude with
His Unborn Child.

I must be strong and carry on
As My Beloved's vitality continues to wane.
In His absence, I will not
Allow His sacrifice to be in vain.

Our God is great;
He is my Beloved Consort, and
I carry the Child of Promise, the
Reborn face of His Father, and
The gift of His return within me.
Any mother must only look
Into her child's eyes to see
That her Beloved companion lives on.

Blessings of the Feast of the Equinox,
Dear Traveler
May the spirit of Mabon
Be with you on your endless journey,
In this world and the Next:
Blessed Be!

The Blessings of Mabon

Blessed Be the Autumnal Equinox
The days are shorter, and the nights are longer
As nature paints a rainbow all around us
One final show before the winter rest.

The coolness of the Autumn breeze
brings a fresh feeling
As we welcome the relief from the summer heat.
The leaves of gold, orange, and brown
Drop to the earth and whisper beneath our feet.

Our children have returned to school, and
are learning and growing
And the season of celebrations now begins.
We prepare for the winter from our bounty
Of the spring and the summer.
We give thanks for the abundance in our lives!

Archangel Michael

Hail to the Archangel Michael
Champion warrior of Heaven and Earth
The right hand of the Elohim,
Warrior of the Highest
Swift of word and deed.

In the absence of the Solar Lord
Michael holds the Sword
Balancing the Scales of
Justice with Might
Peace with Courage.

Michael, You inspire me to
Live heartily, choose wisely, and
Fill our hearts with gratitude and reverence.
I turn to you, Archangel Michael,
Powerful protector and guide.

On this day of Mabon,
I give thanks for your unwavering presence,
Your strength and courage.
Defender of the faith,
Who fights darkness and negativity.

Archangel Michael,
I offer my heartfelt thanks for your guidance,
Protection and blessings.
I strive to bring healing, love, and
Balance into the world on this Equinox.

Kyriat of the Feast

The Day of Enlightenment
Has come;
The Great Salvation has arrived,
I grasp the Crown of Illumination
When I look within.
I open my eyes to the Unveiled Truth
I am capable of sight for the first time
As the clouds of dogma have lifted.

This Autumn Equinox, with this Feast,
I declare the Cornerstone of my Faith

[The Grains of Corn]
With this offering of Grain
I acknowledge the Solar Lord's
Self-sacrifice
To ensure humanity's abundance

[Pour the Oil]
With this offering of Oil
I acknowledge the Peace
That has now replaced the Turmoil
Of Blindness and Confusion

[Pour the Wine]
With this offering of Wine
I acknowledge the Happiness
That has now replaced the clouds
Of self-doubt and sorrow

The heights of Enlightenment

Are limitless, and
Awareness is the key.
I will continue to excel
The limitations of the flesh.
The oral teachings of the Mysteries
Lie hidden with me,
Reoccurring in every age.

Through immersion in the Spirit,
Returning to the Great Womb of my
Celestial Mother,
Only to be born again.

The Final Feast

I bid farewell to the Wise King
As I stand with the Queen of Heaven
At the Final Feast
Before His journey home:
I await His return.

Grains for the Bread
Are Broken
Fruit of the Vine
Is Shed
Eat of this, and I will never hunger
Drink, and I will never thirst

May the abundance of the Mother
The Bountifulness of the Father
Nourish and sustain me
All the days of my life.

Blessed Be the Trinity

Blessed be the God
Kyrie Eleison!
Blessed be the Goddess

Kyrie Eleison!
Blessed be the Solar Lord
Kyrie Eleison!

Blessings to the God
King of the heavens and cosmos
Father of sustenance and power
Our God of infinite existence

Blessings to the Goddess
Queen of the Earth and Seas
Mother of creation and fortitude
Our Goddess of infinite existence

Blessings to the Solar Son
Prince of peace and love
Son of sacrifice and selflessness
Our Solar Lord of infinite existence

Blessed Be the Trinity
This Kyriat of the Feast
Kyrie Eleison, Kyrie Eleison
Kyrie Eleison!

Raising & Releasing Energy

As above, so below
Between my hands
I feel the energy grow!

To shape, mold, and create
That which only I can facilitate
The Circle Within and
The Circle Without
Neverending energy capable of
Magick and Miracles
From which all things
May be obtained:

So as I will it, So mote it be!

I now release this Energy of Mabon!

The Great Rite

As the Spear to the Cauldron,
The Lance to the Grail
Spirit to Flesh,
The Cakes and the Ale

The Alchemical Wedding
Unites the Lady and Lord;
Love makes One from Two
The Chalice and the Sword.

Feast and Libations

[Hold up the plate of cakes toward the heavens and say:]
On this magickal day of Mabon, I celebrate
And share these cakes, symbolic of the
Grains that sustain my body:
I partake so that I may never hunger.

[Put a portion of the food on a separate plate
as a sign of thanks and communion.]

[Raise a chalice of wine or juice towards the heavens and say:]
On this magickal day of Mabon, I celebrate
and share this drink of the vine,
Symbolic of the blood of life:
I partake so that I may never thirst.
Blessed Be!

[Pour a portion of the wine onto the ground.]

Journal Your Thoughts

Thank the Deities

As this ritual of Mabon draws to a close,
I honor the Elohian Pantheon:
My wondrous Goddess, mighty God, and
Solar Lord Jesus.
Thank you for witnessing this Solar Rite
As You continue to bestow your essence of
Life, love, and renewal each day.
Blessed Be the Trinity!

Dismiss the Quarters

Elements of the Divine
Keepers of the Watchtowers of the North,
Who commands the Earth
Thank you for your presence
This Kyriat of the Feast:
Stay if you will; go if you must
Hail and Farewell!

Elements of the Divine
Keepers of the Watchtowers of the West,
Who commands the Waters
Thank you for your presence
This Kyriat of the Feast:
Stay if you will; go if you must
Hail and Farewell!

Elements of the Divine
Keepers of the Watchtowers of the South,
Who commands Fire
Thank you for your presence
This Kyriat of the Feast:
Stay if you will; go if you must
Hail and Farewell!

Elements of the Divine
Keepers of the Watchtowers of the East,
Who commands the Air
Thank you for your presence
This Kyriat of the Feast:
Stay if you will; go if you must
Hail and Farewell!

Dismiss the Circle

This rite of Mabon has now ended,
As the Wheel of the Year turns onward.
I am thankful for the many blessings
Of this Harvest Feast!

This Circle is open but never broken.
May the peace of the Trinity
Be ever in your heart.
Merry we meet, and merry we part,
'til merry, we meet again!
Blessed Be!

Samhain
October 31

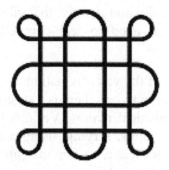

Ritual Correspondences

Altar cloth: Black
Candles: white, black, orange
Herbs: honeysuckle, lavender, mint, roses, feverfew
Stones: amber, jet,
Observances: going through the veil, honoring ancestors, discarding unwanted memories and bad habits
Decorations: pumpkins, gourds, corn stalks, rust and purple mums, bales of hay
Sabbat Mythos: The Goddess mourns her slain consort and Journeys to the Afterlife
Sun position: Sun is 15 degrees Scorpio.
Tarot Card: Death
Rune: Hagalaz
Angel: Azrael

Samhain is celebrated on October 31st, marking the transition between summer's warm, fruitful days and the beginning of winter's darker, colder months. Its origins can be traced back to the ancient Celtic people who inhabited Ireland, Scotland, and Britain. The Celts honored the thinning of the veil between the worlds of the living and the dead, allowing spirits to roam freely among them. Hence, Samhain became a time to honor and communicate with ancestors, seek guidance, and offer thanks for the harvest.

Samhain is the third and final harvest. The Celtic name translates to "summer's end." Spiritually and ritually, this sabbat has many traditional observances; there is no need to feel compelled to perform all the examples included.

During the thinning of the veil, divination and communication rituals are more powerful and effective as there is a stronger connection between the physical and metaphysical realms. Various forms of divination are suggested: tarot card readings, scrying, using a pendulum to dowse for answers, or interpreting tea leaves to gain insights into the coming year or communicate with the spirit realm.

Setting up an ancestor altar adorned with photographs, mementos, and offerings is the best way to pay respects to departed family and friends and seek their guidance and protection. Ancestral spirits can guide, protect, or even warn their living descendants.

A Dumb Supper is a silent meal shared with your ancestors. By symbolically leaving an empty seat at the table, it is an invitation for them to join you. Making an offering of favorite foods is an act of respect and remembrance; including a glass of water and a plate of sugary foods gives energy, allowing them to stay in our realm longer. Pictures and items belonging to that individual can help to serve as trigger objects.

Trinitarian Wicca views Samhain as the beginning of the spiritual new year, a time of reflection and introspection. It's also a time to release emotions that are no longer beneficial. This is the time for cutting ties and eliminating weaknesses. Farmers once slaughtered the weakest livestock that could not survive the winter. Their feed was then reallocated to the healthy animals, sustaining the herd until spring. This custom evolved into the modern practice of ridding oneself of unwanted habits and weaknesses. The Rite of Paper and Fire acts similarly by writing our undesirable characteristics on a piece of paper and dropping them into the fire. Symbolically, as it burns and turns to ash, so do the individual's unnecessary weights and hindrances.

Samhain serves as a bridge between the past and the present, blending ancient customs with contemporary spiritual practices. This sabbat allows Trinitarian Wiccans to connect with their ancestors, express gratitude for nature's abundance, and embrace the transformative energies.

Consecrate the Area

[Add a pinch of salt to the bowl of water and hold it toward the sky, asking this or similar blessings:]

I call upon the Blessed Trinity to
Consecrate this water and this salt for the
Elemental Purification of this Circle.
Representing my Goddess:
Of the Earth and Water of the Sea
So as I will it, So mote it be!

[Using the flame of a candle, light the incense, and hold it toward the sky, asking this or similar blessings:]

I call upon the Blessed Trinity to
Consecrate this flame and
This incense for the
Elemental Purification of this Circle.
Representing my God:
By Fire and Air, Glory to Thee
So as I will it, So mote It Be!

Elemental Chant

[Chant as you consecrate the Circle:]

Earth, my body;
Water my blood.

Air my breath; and
Fire my spirit.

Cast the Circle

I cast this mystical Circle of power
In this hallowed appointed hour:
Within this Spiritual Vortex
Piercing the veil between this world and the next
Ancient energies come to me
So as I will it, So mote it be!

Call the Quarters

Spirits of Old,
Guardians of the East
Keepers of the Element of Air
I ask for your breezy presence
As Spirits pierce the veil from the Ethereal Realms
Empower me as I honor my ancestors
I invoke thee!
Welcome!

Spirits of Old,
Guardians of the South
Keepers of the Element of Fire
I ask for your fiery presence
As Spirits pierce the veil from the Ethereal Realms
Empower me as I honor my ancestors
I invoke thee!
Welcome!

Spirits of Old,
Guardians of the West
Keepers of the Element of Water
I ask for your flowing presence
As Spirits pierce the veil from the Ethereal Realms

Empower me as I honor my ancestors
I invoke thee!
Welcome!

Spirits of Old,
Guardians of the North
Keepers of the Element of Earth
I ask for your fortitude
As Spirits pierce the veil from the Ethereal Realms
Empower me as I honor my ancestors
I invoke thee!
Welcome!

Invocation of the Blessed Trinity

Blessed Be this day of Samhain
Celebrating the Third Harvest, and
The thinning of the Veil
I invoke the Blessed Trinity:

Sacred Mother, Queen of the Earth and Seas
Mother of creation and life
Our Goddess of infinite existence

Divine Father, King of the Heavens and Cosmos
Father of sustenance and power
Our God of endless presence

Solar Lord, Prince of Peace and Charity
Son of sacrifice and selfless love
Our Solar Lord of radiant immortality:
Be with me to experience the
Magick and the Mysteries
In this Rite of Samhain
I Invoke Thee
Welcome!

The Blessings of Samhain

*The gates between the worlds swing open wide and
Our ancestors bid us welcome.
Pumpkins with candles cast shadows on the wall
The crisp chill in the air is autumn's call.*

*Rustling leaves of gold, orange, and brown
The last harvest ends with frost on the ground.
In the cool embrace of autumn's twilight hour,
We gather to honor Samhain's power.*

*The veil grows thin between the worlds we tread,
As we remember the departed, with reverence, not dread.*

*Samhain, a festival of shadows and reflection,
We embrace the darkness without hesitation.
For in this sacred season, we find solace and release,
As we honor the endless cycles of life and find inner peace.*

*The colored leaves fall like whispers from the past,
As we gather around the bonfire, shadows are cast.
We remember our ancestors, their wisdom and grace,
Their spirits linger in this sacred space.*

*Samhain is a time to honor the thinning veil,
As we commune with spirits without fail.
We light the candles, their flames flickering bright,
Guiding lost souls towards the eternal light.*

*In this season of introspection, we turn our gaze within,
Exploring the depths of our souls, where secrets begin.
We shed our masks, revealing our true selves,
Embracing our shadows, where inner wisdom dwells.*

*Samhain celebrates the cycle of life and death,
To honor the lessons learned with each passing breath.
We gather in circles, sharing stories untold,
Creating a tapestry of memories, both new and old.*

In this sacred space, we find comfort and release,
As we honor the departed and find inner peace.
We celebrate the blessings of Samhain's embrace,
And honor the cycles of life with reverence and grace.

May the energy of this season guide us through,
The night's wisdom and insight in all that we do.
With the blessings of Samhain, we find our way,
As we honor the sacredness of this autumnal day.

The Goddess Speaks

Merry Meet Traveler
Please walk with me as
I escort the Aging Sun
One last time into the West.
His Resting Place
In love, comfort, and peace
There, He will regain His vitality
Reborn as the Child of Promise
Who will again take the throne
As my Consort, and
Once more, be at my side.

Come! It is time to descend
Into the Underworld.
Take my Transforming hand,
Let me guide you as we
Walk through passages that are
Unfamiliar to the living but
Are a part of the cycle of life.
Allow fear and trepidation to fall away,
For they have no place here.

With change comes new opportunities,
New life and new dreams.
Let this day of the New Year
Reassure you, Traveler

The Circle is never-ending.
Until the longest night,
His boundless grace is
Veiled in my garden
Sustained by eternal love.

Going Through the Veil

[Construct a doorway with a black cloth to simulate the Veil
Between the Two Worlds or the Other Side. Light a single candle to
Illuminate the area behind the veil]

Vigilant Gatekeeper, please open the door.
Open the gate; open the way!
I come to you humbly to pass through the veil.

I call to my ancestors: blood to blood,
I bring a photo, a glass of water,
And a plate of your favorite foods.
Dine with me tonight!
Impart the wisdom you wish to me,
I will eagerly await any words you whisper
Any emotions you convey
To take with me after my stay.

We may be separated briefly by this dimension
But we are always connected in
Our hearts, minds, and souls.

Lilith, Goddess of Transformation, speaks:

"Greetings to you, Traveler,
Wisely, you come this night
Seeking the way of Transformation.
I am the Goddess of Change and Progress,
Now is the time to release the weight of the last year.
Do not carry the burden of guilt, stress, and pain
Another day. I will take them from you, but first
You must be willing to let
These things go.

To address your loved ones
You must be free of the shadows of the mind
And the weight of a heavy heart.
You must release them into my hands
Before you take another step,
Tell me, Traveler,
What do you cast off?"

[Remove items of jewelry or clothing]

Anath, Goddess of Protection, speaks:

"My sister, I will lead the Traveler
To the nether realm,
It is a path that I have traveled before, and
One that I know well.

Take my hand now, Traveler
Leave the world of the living,
Be strong of heart and dare to descend.
The power of the Ancients protects you,
Allow your intuition to lead your
Heart and mind:
As I lend you comfort.

Loved ones await!
Do not fear the
Tales of fire and punishment;
You alone control your destiny
In this world and in the next."

[The dove of peace descends from the Heavens, then
takes the form of a beautiful maiden after her wedding night]

The Holy Spirit, Goddess of Proclamation, speaks:

"Now, Dear Traveler,
Take my hand
In this world and in the next,
I am with you.

I offer you reassurance as we
Descend into the Underworld
Where my Beloved Consort resides
Awaiting the birth of the Promised Child.

I will stay here while you commune with your loved ones.
Speak freely with those who have gone before you
Without doubt or fear.
Greet them with an open heart and a smile
May your tears be those of joy,
Loved ones are with family and friends, and
For them, you should grieve no more.

Forgive me, Traveler.
Despite my youthful look,
My age has supplanted me
During our descent,
The cycles of the year touched my sleeve.
I am no longer the Young Maiden and
I have grown tired.
I am the Snow Hag:
My youthful beauty has transformed
Into the wisdom of the ages.
Do not weep.
You will meet me again;
When the sabbat of Yule arrives,
You will know me
By the name, Mary.

It is time for you to return to the Living World
For this is a place of rest and recuperation
After a life filled with joy and pain.
You may visit once a year,
On this night.
When your time comes
To cross through the Veil,
you will have no fear, dread, or doubt.

[Spend 5 to 10 minutes trying to reach a friend or family

members who have moved onward to the next realm]

Return now to all that is familiar
Emerge from the darkness into the light.
Allow the veil to close behind you
Until the same time next year.

The Star of Life

[Cut the apple in half crossways to reveal the hidden star]

The apple is the fruit of Eden,
Symbol of wisdom and veiled knowledge.
When seeking the Truth,
The Ancient Mysteries can be found in
The forbidden fruit of
The Tree of Knowledge of Good and Evil
Veils the Hidden Knowledge of the Goddess

The Rite of Paper and Fire

[Take a piece of paper and write a negative quality about yourself, which you no longer wish to possess.]

I cast away dread, doubt, and dismay
All things that do not inspire:
I write my list, fold my paper,
And toss it into the fire.

"Igne Natura Renovatur Integra"
By Fire, Nature is Perfectly Renewed.
By the Fire of my Will, Ignite the Divine Spark
[Drop the Paper into the Fire]

Glory to the Souls Departed

Tonight, as the barrier between the two realms grows thin,
Spirits walk amongst us once again.

They are family, friends, and foes,
I celebrate for them and do not feel sorrow.

I cast away ire and cast away pride
May the good come to pass and the bad be cast aside.
With the promise of a mystical new year,
May I have good health, good wealth, and be of good cheer.

May my loved ones long departed
Be my special guides
From beyond the grave and from the other side.

Give me strength and courage,
And Knowledge Threefold,
To be diligent and fruitful,
And to achieve my goals.

Every ending is a new beginning,
Just as every beginning has an end.
To one and all eternal:
Blessed Be!

Raising & Releasing Energy

As above, so below
Between my hands
I feel the energy grow!

To shape, mold, and create
That which only I can facilitate
The Circle within and
The Circle without
Neverending energy capable of
Magick and Miracles
From which all things
May be obtained:
So as I will it, So mote it be!

I now release this Energy of Samhain!

The Great Rite

As the Spear to the Cauldron,
The Lance to the Grail
Spirit to Flesh,
The Cakes and the Ale

The Alchemical Wedding
Unites the Lady and Lord;
Love makes One from Two
The Chalice and the Sword.

Feast and Libations

[Hold up the plate of cakes toward the heavens and say:]
On this hallowed day of Samhain, I celebrate and
Honor my ancestors
I share these cakes, symbolic of the
Grains that sustain my body:
I partake so that I may never hunger.

[Put a portion of the food on a separate plate
as a sign of thanks and communion.]

[Raise a chalice of wine or juice towards the heavens and say:]
On this magickal day of Samhain, I celebrate and
Honor my ancestors
I share this drink of the vine,
Symbolic of the blood of life:
I partake so that I may never thirst.
Blessed Be!

[Pour a portion of the wine onto the ground.]

Journal Your Thoughts

Thank the Deities

As this ritual of Samhain draws to a close,
I honor the Elohian Pantheon:
My wondrous Goddess, mighty God, and
Solar Lord Jesus.
Thank you for witnessing this Solar Rite
As You continue to bestow your essence of
Life, love, and renewal each day.
Blessed Be the Trinity!

Dismiss the Quarters

I wish to thank the
Angels and Messengers of the Divine
Spirits, Elements, and Powers
Of the North, who commands the Earth
For being with me
As I celebrate the ethereal Mysteries of Samhain
Stay if you will; go if you must,
Hail and Farewell!

I wish to thank the
Angels and Messengers of the Divine
Spirits, Elements, and Powers
Of the West, who command the Waters
For being with me
As I celebrate the ethereal Mysteries of Samhain
Stay if you will; go if you must
Hail and Farewell!

I wish to thank the
Angels and Messengers of the Divine
Spirits, Elements, and Powers
Of the South, who command the Fire
For being with me
As I celebrate the ethereal Mysteries of Samhain
Stay if you will; go if you must

Hail and Farewell!

I wish to thank the
Angels and Messengers of the Divine
Spirits, Elements, and Powers
Of the East, who commands the Air
For being with me
As I celebrate the Ethereal Mysteries of Samhain
Stay if you will; go if you must
Hail and Farewell!

Dismiss the Circle

This Rite of Samhain has now ended,
The Wheel of the Year turns onward.
I have relinquished my fears
Of the death and embrace the Mysteries:
As Above, So Below
As vast as the Universe,
So is my Soul

This Circle is open but never broken.
May the peace of the Trinity
Be ever in your heart.
Merry we meet, and merry we part,
'til merry, we meet again!
Blessed Be!

Drawing Down the Sun

Drawing Down the Sun is a non-sabbatic Solar Rite. It is a neglected ritual with a similar purpose and benefits to Drawing Down the Moon. Drawing Down the Sun can help align a male's body as women's bodies benefit from Lunar Rites. Drawing Down the Sun should be held on a Sunday, the day of the Sun. Noon is when the Sun is at its zenith. Bonfires are lit in the middle of the Circle.

This ritual order is the same as esbats, sabbats, and kyriats. The one exception is the thanking and dismissing of the Quarters and the Father and the Son; however, do not release the circle at the end of the ceremony. The Circle widens to an area where the Circle members may bring in their families and have a cookout, play games, and enjoy the warmth of the Sun, symbolizing the spiritual passion of God the Father and the Solar Lord. At dusk, douse the bonfire, which dismisses the Sacred Space.

The altar cloths and candle color themes are yellow and orange.

Consecrate the Area

[Add a pinch of salt to the bowl of water and hold it
toward the sky, asking this or similar blessings:]

I call upon the Blessed Trinity to
Consecrate this water and this salt for the
Elemental Purification of this Circle.
Representing my Goddess:
Of the Earth and Water of the Sea
So as I will it, So mote it be!

[Using the flame of a candle, light the incense,
and hold it toward the sky,
asking this or similar blessings:]

I call upon the Blessed Trinity to
Consecrate this flame and
This incense for the
Elemental Purification of this Circle.
Representing my God:
By Fire and Air, Glory to Thee
So as I will it, So mote It Be!

Elemental Chant

[Chant as you consecrate the Circle:]

Earth, my body;
Water my blood.
Air my breath; and
Fire my spirit.

Cast the Circle

O Ancient Circle, the Sphere of the
Ebb and Flow of time
I summon and create thee!
World between worlds

All of the Energies Within:
Assemble thyself, Solar Temple!

Call the Quarters

Hail to the Light Bringers of the East
Lords of the Watchtowers
Keepers of Wind and Air
Come into this Circle and
Empower this Rite
As I Draw Down the Sun
I Invoke thee:
Welcome!

Hail to the Light Bringers of the South
Lords of the Watchtowers
Keepers of Fire and Gnosis
Come into this Circle and
Empower this Rite
As I Draw Down the Sun
I Invoke thee:
Welcome!

Hail to the Light Bringers of the West
Lords of the Watchtowers
Keepers of Water and Emotions
Come into this Circle and
Empower this Rite
As I Draw Down the Sun
I Invoke thee:
Welcome!

Hail to the Light Bringers of the North
Lords of the Watchtowers
Keepers of Earth and Stability
Come into this Circle and
Empower this Rite
As I Draw Down the Sun

I Invoke thee:
Welcome!

The Candlelight Ceremony

[Light the white candle]
God of the Cosmos
Commander of the Stars
He who is Wisdom
The Tree of Life
Open my eyes
I invoke Thee
Welcome!

[Light the red candle]
Solar Lord
Regent of the Sun
He who is Beauty on
The Tree of Life
Open my eyes
I invoke Thee
Welcome!

[Lights the black candle]
Goddess of the Earth
Lunar Queen of the heavens
She, Who is Understanding
On the Tree of Life
Open my eyes
I invoke Thee
Welcome!

Invocation of the Father and Son

Glorious God of the heavens,
Father of the Solar Lord
Lover, Father, and Sage

> *With the Sun, I do align*
> *O God within me, O God without*
> *How can I ever be in doubt?*
>
> *There is no place where I may go*
> *And not there see God's face, not know*
> *I am God's vision and God's ears*
> *So, through the harvest of my years*
> *I am the Sower and the Sown*
> *God's Self-unfolding and God's Own.*
>
> *I ask for your presence*
> *From the heavens above*
> *Come into this Circle*
> *Showering me with Your Love*

Charge of the God

> *Listen, not with your ears,*
> *But with your Elohian mind!*
> *To the wise words of the Eternal God*
> *Who is known by many names:*
> *El, Yahweh, Adonai, Elohim, El Shaddai*
> *Jesus, the Logos*
>
> *Dance and sing my praises,*
> *Your Elohian Grand Creator*
> *Rejoice in my presence,*
> *And listen to my words, my music!*
> *Call forth the seasons on the winds of time*
> *As I dance and frolic among the meadows.*
>
> *I am that I am, Father of all living things*
> *I am witness to the knowledge of life everlasting*
> *I hold the keys to the Gates of Heaven*
> *And speak the secrets of regeneration.*
> *I bear the wings of death upon my back*
> *And judge with the laws of harmony intact*

The blood of sacrifice drips from my brow
As the cycle of rebirth abounds
Eternally linked I am to you, any living creation
A circle unbroken brought forth from my imagination

Drawing Down the Sun

Now I will
Draw Down the Sun
I raise my hands to
Feel the Divine essence of the God
As it flows into my fingertips,
Causing warm tingles
Coursing down my arms
Into my body
Igniting my heart and soul.

I hold my hands skyward
To the heavens
To feel your Fatherly touch
I invoke the Blessed Elohim
Gods of all Life:
Cosmos, Sun, and Fire...

By Bud and by seed
By stem and by root
By Leaf and By Flower and Fruit
By Life and By Love
I invoke Thee to
Descend into this Circle
Into your children
Into the bodies of your children,
Your Priests and Priestess:
Great Solar Father of All
I Invoke Thee!

Blessed Be my feet

That has brought me in these ways
[Anoint feet with oil]

Blessed Be my knees
That shall kneel at the sacred altar
[Anoint knees with oil]

Blessed Be my womb/phallus
Without which, we could not create
[Anoint abdomen with oil]

Blessed Be my breast/chest
Formed in Beauty / Strength
[Anoint chest with oil]

Blessed Be my lips
That shall utter the Sacred Names
[Anoint lips with oil]

[Speak the names aloud]
El! Yahweh! Adonai!
Elohim! El Shaddai!
Jesus! The Logos!

Psalms of the Father and Son

Ever as I pass through the ways
Do I feel the presence
Of the Father and the Son
I know that in ought I do
They are with me,
They abide in me,
And I am in them, forever.

No Evil shall be entertained.
For purity is the Dweller
Within me and about me
For good, do I strive
And for good do I live.
Love unto all things.

So be it, forever.

Raising & Releasing Energy

As above, so below
Between my hands
I feel the energy grow!

To shape, mold, and create
That which only I can facilitate
The Circle Within and
The Circle Without
Neverending energy capable of
Magick and Miracles
From which all things
May be obtained:
So as I will it, So mote it be!

I now release this Energy of this Solar Rite!

The Great Rite

As the Spear to the Cauldron,
The Lance to the Grail
Spirit to Flesh,
The Cakes and the Ale

The Alchemical Wedding
Unites the Lady and Lord;
Love makes One from Two
The Chalice and the Sword.

Feast and Libations

[Hold up the plate of cakes toward the heavens and say]
On this radiant day of the Sun, I celebrate!
I give thanks to God, Goddess, and Solar Lord

For the cakes, symbolic of the
Grains that sustain my bodies
Throughout the Wheel of the Year!

[Put a portion of the food on a separate plate
as a sign of thanks and communion.]

[Raise a chalice of wine or juice towards the heavens and say:]
Likewise, on this radiant day of the Sun
I share this drink of thanks and honor
God, Goddess, and Solar Lord
I align myself with the Sun, the Moon, and the Earth!
Blessed Be!

[Pour a portion of the wine onto the ground.]

Journal Your Thoughts

Thank the Deities

As this ritual of the Sun ends,
I honor the Elohian Pantheon:
My wondrous Goddess, mighty God, and
Solar Lord Jesus.
Thank you for witnessing this Solar Rite
As You continue to bestow your essence of
Life, love, and renewal each day.
Blessed Be the Trinity!

Dismiss the Quarters

Light Bringers of the North,
Lords of the Watchtowers
Keepers of Earth
I thank you for your presence!
Stay if you will; go if you must
Hail and Farewell!

Light Bringers of the West,
Lords of the Watchtowers
Keepers of the Waters
I thank you for your presence!
Stay if you will; go if you must
Hail and Farewell!

Light Bringers of the South,
Lords of the Watchtowers
Keepers of Fire
I thank you for your presence!
Stay if you will; go if you must
Hail and Farewell!

Light Bringers of the East,
Lords of the Watchtowers
Keepers of Air
I thank you for your presence!
Stay if you will; go if you must
Hail and Farewell!

Dismiss the Circle
[The Circle is Closed when the balefire is doused]

The History of the Pentacle

"Men never do evil so completely and
Cheerfully, as when they do it from
Religious conviction."
Blaise Pascal, Penses (1670)

Despite the Christopagan community's advancement in the last two decades, this chapter remains pertinent to understanding the role of the pentacle in Wicca. The word pentagram comes from the Greek πεντάγραμμον (*pentagrammon*); it is visibly broken into two Greek terms: *pente*, meaning five, and *gramme*, which translates to the line. A pentagram is five lines diagrammed in a manner to create a star.

The Pentacle corresponds with the element of Earth and is an essential tool on a Trinitarian Wiccan altar. It symbolizes the five elements: Air, Fire, Water, Earth, and Spirit. The pentacle is typically created on a flat surface of clay, wood, or resin for an altarpiece. A dish or plate with a star-shaped design is etched or embossed when used in the Cakes and ale ritual. This symbol usually incorporates five points connected by lines to create an image representing the element of Earth and its connection to fertility, divination, and prosperity.

The pentacle and pentagram are often used interchangeably, but there is a difference. The pentagram is a five-pointed star, and the pentacle is the star within a Circle. Unfortunately, the direction of the top point gets a bad reputation. *A Witches' Bible* by Janet and Stewart Farrar explains:

> *"Pentagram – A five-pointed star. An upright pentagram (i.e., with a single point uppermost) represents (1) a human being (astride with arms outstretched) or (2) the four Elements (q.v.) governed by the fifth, Spirit. An inverted pentagram (i.e., with a single point downwards) represents Spirit still subservient to the four Elements. It is commonly perceived as a black magick symbol unless used as the symbol of a second-degree initiate. The implication is that they are still on the way to full development."*

The pentacle has a known history of over 8,000 years and has been used in various ways. In Wicca, the pentacle is a sacred symbol representing the five elements: earth, air, fire, water, and spirit. It is typically depicted as a five-pointed star enclosed within a Circle. The points of the star represent the elements, while the Circle symbolizes unity, wholeness, and protection.

The five-pointed star has a rich and diverse history that predates its association with Wicca. The earliest known depictions of the pentacle can be traced back to ancient Mesopotamia, specifically Sumer and Babylon. It was used as a protective symbol of protection associated with the goddess Ishtar. Approximately 3,500 rulers in Ancient Mesopotamia used the five-pointed star as a military symbol, indicating their political power and achievements.

The Pentalpha was one of Sumer's most utilized sacred symbols with multiple uses within their culture. It appears on clay tablets and cylinder seals circa 3500 BC onward as religious and administrative symbols. The oldest surviving example was found at Uruk and is estimated to date back to 3370 BCE.

In ancient Greek culture, Pythagorean mystics believed in the mystical properties of numbers and considered the pentacle's geometric qualities the symbol of perfection, mathematically and metaphysically. Pythagoreans hypothesized that the number five is the sum of the feminine number two and the masculine three, reinforcing the numerical belief that the microcosm, or humanity, reflects the macrocosm, the Universal Divine.

In Ancient Egypt, the pentacle was associated with the goddess Isis and was believed to have protective and magical properties. It was often painted in tombs or placed on grave goods as a protective symbol for the deceased. The ancient Egyptians also considered it a symbol of health, longevity, and prosperity.

The ancient Jews believed that the pentacle was used by King Solomon to bind demons and protect him from evil spirits. The pentacle's five points represent the Five Books of Moses (the Pentateuch), which contain the core teachings of Jewish law. It is sometimes called the Seal of Solomon or the Star of David. One use of the symbol of protection from harm and evil. The six-pointed hexagram known as the Star of David is also associated with Judaism. Some scholars believe it may have been developed in conjunction with the pentacle. In contrast, others argue they are entirely unrelated symbols.

It has since become a powerful protective symbol for many followers of monotheistic faiths, including Christians, Muslims, and Jews. According to some religious historians, the five-pointed star likely predates its association with King Solomon. Other ancient cultures, such as Sumerians or Babylonians, may have used it.

The five-pointed star entered Christianity through the writings of St. Augustine. He compared it to the five wounds of the Biblical Jesus. He hypothesized that early Christians might have used it to identify each other. St. Augustine also associated it with the five virtues: justice, temperance, wisdom, fortitude, and charity. Additionally, early Christians affiliated the pentacle with the Biblical Jesus's five wounds during the crucifixion until medieval times. The pentacle's visibility diminished during the Inquisition, fearing the Church's persecution.

During the Renaissance, the pentacle gained popularity with ceremonial magicians and occultists. It was used in their rituals and in the creation of talismans. These practitioners believed that the pentacle could be used to obtain power, shield against evil forces, and provide protection from harm.

In the late 19th century, the Hermetic Order of the Golden Dawn drew on elements from Western mystical and occult traditions to create its own system of magical practice. This system incorporated the pentacle as one of its primary symbols for ritual magic, invoking different elements depending on how it was drawn.

By the early 20th century, the pentacle had been adopted into Western esotericism among Wiccans, Pagans, and the Craft. The pentacle is used during rituals to focus energy and invoke the elements while maintaining a connection with the divine. The lower four pentacle points represent the physical world's elements: earth, air, fire, and water. The top point represents Spirit.

The early philosophers of India, led by the sage Patanjali, rationally correlated the five points on the star to represent the senses through which stimulus information enters the mind: sight, smell, taste, touch, and hearing. The center of the pentacle was thought to stand for a sixth sense, either the collective unconscious or the spiritual connection between each individual and their Higher Self.

Leonardo da Vinci's iconic sketch, The Vitruvian Man, presents the human body in the center of a circle and square. This image is based on what Vitruvius, an Ancient Roman architect, believed to be a spiritual connection between humans and their universe. He thought that if humanity could comprehend the soul within us, they would understand the universe, as both are equally grand. The picture captures this concept by illustrating a body inside a square and a circle.

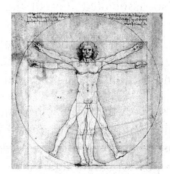

The relationship between the pentacle and the Church is intriguing. Newly Christianized, Constantine still saw himself as a god. He chose to use the pentagram on his own seal and amulet, and many in Roman society followed suit with its usage. When the Church of Rome was born, Helena, Constantine's mother, wanted to adorn it with the cross instead of the ancient pentacle. Legend explains that while traveling in the Holy Land, she discovered the same cross Jesus had been crucified in a cave believed to house his resurrection tomb.

The True Cross was a powerful symbol of devotion, faith, and protection to the early Christians. It exemplified Jesus's sacrifice and strength in Christianity. When reported, Constantine had the cross taken to Jerusalem and placed in the Church of the Holy Sepulcher.

The powerful icon remained until 614 A.C.E. when Chosroes II of Persia captured Jerusalem and moved the cross to his homeland for thirteen years. The Roman Emperor Heraclius defeated Chosroes and reclaimed the cross, placing it in Constantinople before returning it to Jerusalem. It was believed to be hidden by the Christians in 1009 C.E., remaining concealed until the First Crusade in 1099, when it would be used as a religious banner, symbolizing power and strength against their enemies. The Crusaders succeeded in reclaiming the holy city from Muslim rule, allowing Christianity to remain permanent through this everlasting symbol of faith.

The pentacle has been a vital icon throughout history. It has connotations with mystical powers and Divine connections between humanity and God. However, its association with Christian symbolism is debatable compared to its roots in Eastern religious beliefs such as Taoism or Hinduism. Experts are divided on whether it was a sacred instrument for King Solomon or if it had other ancient meanings prior to its usage within Judaism or Christianity.

Regardless of where it originated, what remains is that humanity can embrace its power and protection through faith while still utilizing reason and logic simultaneously, just as Vitruvius suggested centuries ago when creating his masterpiece depicting the human body's divine position within a Circle surrounded by a pentacle-shaped star. Herein lies our connection between heaven and earth: maintaining a balanced relationship between our internal spirit and our external reality provides immense power. Both realms must collaborate perfectly and equally to achieve enlightenment and spiritual completion.

References & Suggested Reading

Adler, Margot, *Drawing Down The Moon: Witches, Druids, Goddess-Worshippers, and Other Pagans in America*, Penguin Books, 2006.

Berg, Rav P. S., *The Essential Zohar: The Source of Kabbalistic Wisdom*, Bell Tower/Random House, New York, New York, 2002.

Borg, Marcus J., *Meeting Jesus Again for the First Time: The Historical Jesus & the Heart of Contemporary Faith*, HarperSanFrancisco, San Francisco, California, 1995.

Campbell, Joseph, *The Hero with A Thousand Faces*, Bollingen Press, New Jersey, 1972.

Chandler Pittman, Nancy, *Christian Wicca: The Trinitarian Tradition*, Authorhouse Publications, Bloomington, Indiana, 2003.

Cooper, Rabbi David A., *God Is A Verb: Kabbalah and the practice of mystical Judaism*, Riverhead Books, New York, 1997.

Farrar, Janet, and Stewart, *A Witches' Bible: A Complete Witches' Handbook*, Phoenix Publishing Inc., Blaine, Washington, 1984.

_____, The Witches' Goddess, Phoenix Publishing Inc., Blaine, Washington, 1987.

_____, The Witches' God, Phoenix Publishing Inc. Blaine, Washington, 1989.

Freke, Timothy, and Gandy, Peter, *The Jesus Mysteries: Was the "Original Jesus" a Pagan God?* Three Rivers Press, London, UK, 1999.

_____, Jesus and the Lost Goddess: The Secret Teachings of the Original Christians, Harmony, 2002.

Gardner, Gerald B., *The Meaning of Witchcraft*, Mercury Publishing, Lake Toxaway, North Carolina, 1959 – 1999.

Graves, Robert, *The White Goddess*, Farrar, Straus, and Giroux, New York, New York, 1948.

Grazer, James G., *The Golden Baugh,* Avenel Books, New York, 1890, 1981.

Hall, Manly P., *The Secret Teachings of All Ages,* Jovian Press, 1928.

_____, The Ancient Mysteries and Secret Societies, Jovian Press,

Jackson, John G., *Pagan Origins of the Christ Myth,* Girard & Stewart, 1941.

Kuhn, Ph.D., Alvin Boyd, S*hadow of the Third Century, A Revaluation of Christianity,* Academy Press, Elizabeth, New Jersy, 1949.

Levi, Eliphas, *The Key of the Mysteries,* Weiser, 1861.

Lewis, Spencer H., *Mystical Life of Jesus,* (AMORC), 1929.

Massey, Gerald, *The Historical Jesus and the Mythical Christ,* Book Tree, Escondido, CA, 2000.

Mead, G. R. S*., Fragments of a Forgotten Faith: A Contribution to the Study of the Origins of Christianity*, University Books, New Hyde Park, New York, 1960.

McCoy, Edain, *The Sabbats: A Witch's Approach to Living the Old Ways,* Llewellyn Publications, St. Paul, Minnesota, 2002.

Morrison, Dorothy, *The Craft: A Witch's Book of Shadows*, Llewellyn Publications, St. Paul, Minnesota, 2001.

Murray, Margret, *The God of the Witches*, Oxford University Press, New York, 1931.

Pagel, Elaine, *The Gnostic Gospels,* Random House, New York, 1981.

Patai, Raphael, *The Hebrew Goddess*, The Wayne State University Press, 1967.

Pike, Albert, *Morals, and Dogma of the Ancient and Accepted Rite of Scottish Freemasonry*, Global Grey, 1957.

Regardie, Israel, *The Golden Dawn: A Complete Guide in Ceremonial Magic,* Llewellyn Publications, St. Paul, Minnesota, 2002.

Sanders, Alex, and Baker, J.W., *The Alex Sanders Lectures,* Magickal Childe Publishing, Inc. New York, New York, 1984.

Shadwyn, *The Crafted Cup: Ritual Mysteries of the Goddess and the Grail,* Llewellyn Publications, St. Paul, Minnesota, 1994.

Starhawk, *The Spiral Dance: A Rebirth of the Ancient Religion of the Great Goddess,* Harper & Row Publishers, Inc., New York, New York, 1979.

Spiritual Renewal, Theosophical Publishing House, Wheaton, Illinois, 2007.

About the Author

Nancy Chandler is a ChristoPagan Witch, author, and practitioner/founder of Trinitarian Wicca. Born July 4th, Nancy has always been an independent thinker and a spiritual rebel. After a career as a professional musician and songwriter for multiple bands, she founded Delinquent Records USA in 1987. Nancy toured the United States full-time with her various bands, frequently appearing in major magazines and independent publications worldwide.

In the 2000s, Nancy owned and operated an occult store called *Shadows and Light Shoppe.* Her business included classes on Wicca, ceremonial magick, and Hoodoo. It stocked a large selection of items for the entire magickal community. Nancy is a B.O.T.A. studied empathic tarot reader and continues to read professionally at New Age Festivals. She is a member of the Fellowship of Isis and continues her metaphysical studies with the Ancient Mystical Order Rosae Crucis (AMORC). In her spare time, Nancy enjoys engaging in paranormal research and has become an enthusiast for Unidentified Aerial Phenomena (UAP).

Made in the USA
Las Vegas, NV
30 November 2024